T0311312

The Dark Eclipse

The Dark Eclipse

Reflections on Suicide and Absence

A. W. BARNES

Bucknell UNIVERSITY | BUCKNELL UNIVERSITY PRESS

Lewisburg, Pennsylvania

Library of Congress Cataloging-in-Publication Data

Names: Barnes, Andrew William, 1963– author.
Title: The dark eclipse : reflections on suicide and absence / A.W. Barnes.
Description: Lewisburg, Pennsylvania : Bucknell University Press, [2019] |
Identifiers: LCCN 2018044944 (print) | LCCN 2018046222 (ebook) |
ISBN 9781684480449 (epub) | ISBN 9781684480463 (web PDF) | ISBN
9781684480425 (cloth : alk. paper) | ISBN 9781684480432 (pbk. : alk. paper)
Subjects: LCSH: Barnes, Mike, –1993. | Barnes, Andrew William, 1963– |
Suicide victims—United States. | Gay men—Family relationships—United States.
Classification: LCC HV6548.U5 (ebook) | LCC HV6548.U5 B37 2019 (print) |
DDC 362.28092—dc23
LC record available at https://lccn.loc.gov/2018044944

978-1-68448-000-5 (cloth)

A British Cataloging-in-Publication record for this book is available
from the British Library.

Two of the essays in this book have appeared, in different edited forms, in the
following publications: "Familial Bodies" in *Broad Street*, and "*Morta Sicura*" in *Away*.

♾ The paper used in this publication meets the requirements of the American
National Standard for Information Sciences—Permanence of Paper for Printed
Library Materials, ANSI Z39.48-1992.

www.bucknell.edu/UniversityPress

Manufactured in the United States of America

DCCF

How great love is, presence best tryall makes,
But absence tryes how long this love will bee;
　　To take a latitude
　　Sun, or starres, are fitliest view'd
　　At their brightest, but to conclude
Of longitudes, what other way have wee,
But to marke when, and where the darke eclipses bee?

　　—John Donne, from "Valediction to his booke"

Mom & Dad & the rest of my loving family & friends:
I love you all so dearly. I hate the pain that this will cause you. My only response can be that my own personal pain is just overwhelming. I fought so hard all my life to give myself the self-esteem I needed to survive emotionally as a gay man in this society, then to have a devastating disease come along & rob me of all my self worth is just too much. I wish I were more like you dad who can attribute it all to God's will & get on with it. I think God is all that matters as well as family. Mom, I have loved & adored you so much. You are a perfect & wonderful person. There is nothing I wouldn't give to live as a married man in Indianapolis with all of you. I enjoyed you so much. I love you all so much.

My life is nothing without you. You guys are so special to me. I was so fortunate to grow up with such a wonderful family. The best family a man can ask for. My nieces and nephews are so precious.

You may not understand but I can't but so my heart's desire is to live in Indy & be married ou are very spal people th his &

Contents

The Dark Eclipse

A Complaint

The Midtown North Police Precinct in Manhattan is located at 306 W. Fifty-Fourth Street between Eighth and Ninth Avenues. It's a four-story limestone building in the art deco style of Rockefeller Center. The windows, however, look cheap: thin metal frames and single-paned sashes, some of which are propped open with pieces of wood. In a few of the windows there are air conditioners that drip water down the front of the building and stain the façade. An oversized American flag is supported by a sturdy-looking metal pole bolted to the front of the building. The flag hangs low over the sidewalk. The precinct has two doors, both metal and painted an algae green. The doors are set back in a portal with angular ornamentation along the lintel. Above the door on the right in silver plates is the precinct's number (18th), and above the door on the left it reads "Office."

Despite the obvious signage, I'm standing across the street trying to decide which door to enter. I've been standing here for over fifteen minutes.

It's my shrink's idea to come here. He thinks that I lack the desire or the initiative to look squarely at the facts of my past and determine what is true and what has been distorted by time.

A police cruiser rolls down the street and turns into an alleyway next to the building, driving down a ramp to the back of the building where, I imagine, people who have been arrested are brought into the precinct building.

It's a damp day in early May of 2015. My skin feels clammy beneath my work shirt and wool pants. I don't know whether to unzip my coat to get some air beneath my clothes or button up the coat collar to keep the dampness out.

A young guy in a graying T-shirt and a patchy beard walks a bulldog down the block toward me. The dog zigzags from one side of the sidewalk to the other, sniffing the edges of stoops and around trees and at the bottom of trash bags piled up on the curb. The guy is talking on his cellphone and doesn't pay attention to either the dog or to me. When they reach me, I have to step off the curb and into the street between two black sedans in order to let them pass.

I can't decide which door of the precinct to enter because I'm trying to recall a memory that has become cloudy over the years. I've been to this building before: twenty-two years ago, after my older brother Mike died. I was with my parents then, and we'd come to collect Mike's personal effects: his watch and eyeglasses and wallet and address book. We entered through one of these doors. It seems important to remember which one if I want the memory of that day to come back to me clearly.

It was a Saturday in late October of 1993. Mike's body had been found in a hotel room in Times Square, which is part of the 18th Precinct. I was living in Minneapolis and flew in that Friday, spending the night in Mike's apartment. My parents had flown in that morning from Indianapolis, the hometown where Mike and I grew up.

My parents and I had met at the medical examiner's office to identify Mike's body, and then we headed across town to the 18th Precinct building. It was midmorning and traffic coming up First Avenue was sparse. My mother and I crossed against the light; she'd wrapped herself around my arm. My father, however, refused to move and stood stoically on the sidewalk on the east side of the avenue.

"There are laws for a reason," my father said when the light changed and he caught up to us.

My mother and I pretended as if we hadn't heard my father, like children ignoring an annoying sibling.

I had a sense that my mother had spent most of her married life ignoring my father, who, before they married, was studying to be a Trappist monk. The vow of celibacy was obviously too much for him. He overreacted to this failure, I thought, by fathering seven sons and one daughter—my older brothers Tony, Joe, and Mike; my younger brothers Eddy, Rob and Pat; and, my only sister Marie and me stuck in the middle. Marie was twenty-three months older than I was. Eight children born within the span of eleven years from 1957 to 1968, a time when strict Catholics like my parents believed that birth control was an affront to God and the Church.

My father may have left the monastery, I thought, but not monasticism. I've had to learn to put aside the lessons he tried to teach me—moral rectitude, a myopic worldview, an intolerance for difference.

Before we went to the police station, we stopped for lunch at a restaurant patronized by tourists who liked fried mozzarella sticks and nachos and over-dressed Caesar salads. It wasn't yet noon and the restaurant was empty. We sat in a plywood booth. It was a dark and cavernous place that smelled of cigarette smoke and wet carpet.

As she nearly always did back then, my mother wore a light-blue windbreaker, which she took off and hung on a hook next to the booth. She also wore pleated khakis and a pale blue Gap sweater over a white polo shirt with a collar that had curled under. After hanging up her windbreaker, she scooted into the booth.

My father wore almost the identical outfit, although his windbreaker was off-white and his Gap sweater was pale yellow. He too hung up his jacket, and then scooted in opposite my mother.

I wore black jeans and a green T-shirt. I was muscular and proud of my body, then—I was twenty-nine years old. In the gay community it was normal for us to wear jeans and T-shirts, regardless of the occasion: a night out at the club, a Sunday morning brunch, a funeral.

I sat in the booth next to my mother.

"I'll tell you this much," my father said as we waited for someone to take our order. "I get his money."

My father had a nose that looked permanently swollen as if it'd been broken a few times and never set properly. This caused him to speak from the back of his throat so that, at times, it was difficult to understand what he was saying. (My mother constantly called him out for muttering, which angered my father and caused him to shout at her.) When he made a claim on Mike's money, I heard him clearly.

I wanted to believe that my father's greed was a sign of his grief. I wanted to believe that losing a son had made him angry, and that his anger had made him unexpectedly small. I told myself that he was in shock and didn't know what he was saying. But still, my hands were shaking. I wanted to grab his shoulders and say that fathers aren't supposed to say these things about their dead sons.

I kept silent for a while. What did he expect me to say, anyway? Was he itching for a fight, for me to call him out on such an inappropriate comment? Did he expect me to take him to task the way Mike used to when we were younger?

The waitress finally showed up to take our order.

I blamed my father for Mike's death. I still do. Mike and I grew up as gay sons in a household where my father's unbearable ethics made it impossible for us to live there. In order to survive, Mike and I both abandoned Indianapolis—he moved to New York and I bounced from city to city until I, too, landed in New York a few years after Mike died. Although we no longer lived under my father's oppressive influence, the weight of our upbringing was difficult to carry. Even now after Mike's been dead for a long time and I have lived more years away from Indianapolis than I lived there, I feel a tightening in my chest when I think of my father.

As we waited in the booth for our food, my mother leaned her body into mine. She'd spent most of my childhood doing this. It was obvious to her early on that my father and I would always be at odds—I was a sensitive boy who was nothing like him. My father was tough and dispassionate. My mother would periodically rub my back or run her fingers through my hair. We'd stand next to each other in the church pew dutifully giving our liturgical responses and she'd wrap her pinky around mine.

I don't know if my mother ever did these things for Mike. I don't think she did. Mike was abrasive and offensive like the rest of my five brothers. But lately I've come to think that Mike's aggressive nature was an act he adopted in order to protect himself.

I couldn't bear sitting across from my father in the restaurant. I wanted to believe that when Mike died he left me with a little bit of the courage he had to stand up to my father. To tell my father, for example, that I'd dreamt of being a writer since I was a boy. We didn't come from a family of writers, or one that appreciated writers—or any kind of artist. I was sure that if I made this declaration to my father, he'd laugh at me.

"Perhaps we should give it to charity," I suggested about Mike's money. I sat on my hands to stop them from shaking. "Like God's Love We Deliver."

Beneath the table, my mother placed her hand on top of my thigh.

"What's that?" my father asked. He'd taken the salt and pepper shakers and placed them in front of him, as if he were claiming ownership of them.

"A charity," I repeated, "that helps people who are sick."

"What kind of people?"

I didn't answer him. God's Love We Deliver was a charity established to bring food to gay men who were shut in their apartments and dying of AIDS. My father believed that homosexuality was a choice made by immoral people who had fallen so far from grace that they were a lost cause. My father believed this even of his own gay sons.

"We can talk about this later," my mother said.

My mother took her hand away and rearranged the silverware in front of her. My father pulled out a napkin from a metal dispenser on the table and laid it in his lap. A busboy came by and set glasses of ice water in front of each of us. I took a gulp of water from mine.

"I'm determined to live my own life," I said suddenly. "I don't feel as if I owe it to anybody to live a certain way."

"That's right, darling," my mother said, rubbing my back.

"You owe something to me," my father said. I wasn't looking at my father but instead across the empty restaurant. If I looked at him, I was sure that I'd lose my nerve.

"That's not how I see it," I said.

"Well, you see a lot of things wrong," my father told me.

"I'm my own person," I insisted, looking down at my silverware.

"You are, indeed," my mother said. She folded her hands in her lap and looked at my father as if she were trying to prevent him from doing anything rash.

"The problem with this country," my father said, "is that people have forgotten that a debt has always got to be repaid."

My father came from a long line of hardworking men, of railroad workers and boilermakers, who had in turn descended from Scottish laborers. He grew up in Indianapolis with no money and little hope of escaping the blue-collar lives of his father and grandfather. But he had been tough and self-reliant, going to college on an athletic scholarship, and, after serving in the Korean War, finding a job as a gym teacher. He raised a family of eight children on a gym teacher's salary and an ethics of self-sufficiency. He was a Reagan Republican through and through. My father was a man who pulled himself up by his own bootstraps and had little pity for anyone who couldn't do the same.

"That's enough, Frank," my mother said.

"It's not right," my father said. "It's simply not right."

The waitress returned with our order.

We ate as if we were starving.

Given our history and the improbability of changing my relationship with my father, when Mike died I thought I'd have the chance to fix things with my father. Couldn't Mike's death be the necessary jolt that closed the chasm between us? Couldn't my father and I put aside whatever religious or political convictions we held in order to accept one another as we were? At the very least, I wanted my father to give up his belief that being gay was a death sentence.

When he was finished eating, my father pushed his plate away. It bumped into my mother's and she looked at him as if he'd kicked her under the table. My father looked around for the waitress. He saw the busboy and tried to get his attention by snapping his fingers. The busboy ignored him. My father took a sip of his water and tightened his face as if the water were stale.

"It's not your fault," I said under my breath, hoping that only my mother would hear me.

"Damn right it's not," my father said, thinking that I was speaking to him.

Unlike my father, my mother blamed herself for Mike's death—she had told me this when I spoke with her on the phone before my parents flew to New York. My mother looked at me now. Her eyes watered. If we were alone, I thought, she'd ask me how I could be certain Mike's death wasn't her fault. She'd ask me to help her understand what had happened. She'd ask for forgiveness. I would hold her hand and say that it was going to be all right, that grief was bound to subside and leave behind just a trace of what she was feeling at the moment. I hoped that this would be true for me as well.

"Excuse me!" my father yelled across the restaurant. The busboy looked at my father but didn't respond immediately. Instead, he took a large glass of something from the waiter's stand and took a long drink before heading over to our table.

"Can you tell our waitress to bring our check," my father said when he arrived.

The busboy gathered up our empty plates in silence and retreated into the kitchen.

My father pulled out his wallet and placed it squarely on the table in front of him.

Before the bill arrived, I stood up and allowed my mother to slip out of the booth. She took her jacket from the hook and put it on.

"We'll be outside," she said to my father. I followed her out of the restaurant.

"He doesn't mean it," my mother said as we stood on the sidewalk. She took out a balled up Kleenex from her jacket pocket and wiped her nose. "He's just angry."

My mother was tougher than I ever gave her credit for being. If my father is to be lauded for having raised eight children on a gym teacher's salary, my mother was the one who bore us one after the other with barely a respite, seeming always to have been pregnant, as every photo of our childhoods attests. She was the one at home feeding us, changing our diapers, bathing us, washing our clothes, comforting us when we were ill or aggrieved, scolding us when we misbehaved. She took the brunt of the force that eight children packed so closely together in age inevitably brings.

"We should talk about this," I said, reaching up and rubbing her shoulders as if I were suddenly the caregiver in our relationship.

"We will," she said. She placed her palms flat on my chest, and I lowered my arms. "But not now."

My father came out of the restaurant, struggling to get his jacket on. He had his right arm in the jacket sleeve, but couldn't get his hand back far enough to get the left arm in. My mother helped him.

I hailed a cab.

In 1993, when my parents and I arrived in front of the 18th Precinct on W. Fifty-Fourth Street, I assume that we went into the door marked "Office." I assume that we walked up to the desk sergeant and told him why we were there. Perhaps he already knew we were coming to collect Mike's belongings—the medical examiner's office might have called ahead.

Standing across the street now in 2015, however, the moment when we entered the precinct that day is blank. I remember everything else from that day in vivid detail, but not that moment. Rather it *feels* as if someone met us in front of the building and took us inside without us having to choose an entrance. Perhaps they took us through the door marked "18th" or, more unlikely, down the ramp behind the building.

Instead, my memory of the police precinct back in 1993 begins deep inside the building as a woman police officer grabs my elbow and pulls me into her office while another officer escorts my parents into another room.

I remember the office being crowded: stacks of paper piled high on the officer's desk, overfilled metal bookshelves, reams of paper and forms stacked on top of filing cabinets. The officer asked me to sit in a metal chair.

I was confused. I thought for a second that I'd done something wrong, as if I were responsible for Mike's death. I did feel guilty. I was Mike's only gay sibling. I told myself that I should've done something to save him. But Mike and I didn't have the kind of relationship where he'd ever turn to me for help.

The officer hadn't pulled me aside to place blame.

"Your brother left a note," the officer said. She rubbed her thigh aggressively as if she were trying to remove a stain. "A really nice note. Your parents will appreciate it."

Sitting in front of the officer, I didn't understand what she was saying or why she was saying it to me. Did she think that I'd be better equipped to deal with Mike's death than my parents? Perhaps, I told myself, she'd assumed that I lived in New York and was used to urban brutality.

"In the note," she continued, taking a pad of paper from a pile on her desk, "he says he's gay, and that he was HIV positive."

She handed me the pad of paper that Mike had written his note on. I hadn't known that Mike was HIV positive. I was upset to have learned it first from his note. What was the point of being gay brothers, I thought, if he couldn't confide in me that he had the virus?

"Did your parents know about your brother?" she asked.

I didn't answer her. I wanted to say, "No, we aren't the kind of family that shares intimate details," but then I thought she wouldn't have cared. She was only trying to figure out how to handle a difficult situation.

I read the note as she stood above me. I knew it was Mike's handwriting the moment I saw it; the crisp and exact cursive letters that I'd seen on the occasional birthday card.

The officer was right. The note would please my parents, especially my father. In the note, Mike disavowed being gay and expressed the desire to have been married with children, and living back home in Indianapolis—all of the things my father valued, and nothing that I cared about, or that Mike did when he was still alive.

Even though Mike and I weren't particularly close, I thought that we at least shared some fundamental beliefs that were different from the rest of our family. I thought we shared an understanding that it wasn't necessary to have children to lead a happy life. I thought we'd come to see the value in developing our intellects and our interests in order to become our own best selves. I thought we agreed that this life was all we had, and that it was right and noble to pursue our passions and our careers. As I read his note, however, he seemed to so easily toss aside those beliefs for those of our family, which we had rejected. I felt betrayed. I felt angry.

I thrust the pad of paper back at the officer.

"What does it matter now?" I said, standing up and leaving her office. She caught up to me, grabbed my elbow again, and took me into the other room.

My parents were sitting at a metal table. My father had taken off his jacket and hung it on the back of his chair. My mother had kept her jacket on as if it were cold in the room. It wasn't particularly cold. My mother was hugging herself.

"What did you do?" my father asked me, putting his elbows on the table and leaning toward me.

I went and stood next to my mother, thinking that she'd need my protection when she read the note.

"He didn't do anything," the officer said. "I just needed to talk to him for a minute."

The officer gave the note to my father. He read it quickly, scanning the pages without, I thought, really reading what Mike had written. My father's face was expressionless. When he finished, he looked straight ahead, not turning toward my mother or me. He held out the note for my mother. She took it and held the pad of paper with both hands. As she read the note, my mother began to cry. I rubbed her back. Under the table, my father was tapping his foot. My mother read the note several times, looking for clues, I thought, or trying to memorize every word. When she was finished, she held the note out for me but I didn't take it. I couldn't bear to read it again. My mother put the note on the table in front of her.

Another officer came into the room with a plastic bag with Mike's belongings from the hotel room. My mother grabbed the bag and held it to her chest.

My father thanked the police officer and then walked out of the precinct building as my mother and I followed.

My memory of that day ends there.

When my shrink asks me how Mike died, I tell him that Mike checked into a hotel in Times Square, downed a vial of pills, wrote a suicide note, and then lay down in bed and died. My shrink, however, pushes me for details. He asks me what hotel and what kind of pills and who found him and what did they find and when did they find him and who did the police contact first. I don't know any of these details. My shrink asks me why I don't know them, and I tell him that no one has ever told me.

"Go get the police report," my shrink tells me.

"There's a police report?" I ask.

"Of course there is."

I never thought of Mike's suicide as a crime that warranted a police report. Like the rest of my family, I've thought of his suicide as a private tragedy that has to be endured. But unlike them, I've also seen his suicide as a personal indictment on my life that, at times, feels insignificant and unremarkable.

After standing on the sidewalk across the street for nearly half an hour, I finally walk over and pull open the door marked "Office," walk up the steps, and into the precinct building. I feel as if I'm entering a hostile environment, like I've come to confess to some petty crime like jaywalking. I scratch an itch under my chin.

At the top of the stairs there is a small waiting area that is framed by the sergeant's desk and two waist-high swing gates. The sergeant's desk is elevated a few feet so that the officer on duty towers above the place. The swing gates have large "Stop" signs on them, preventing anyone from passing through them. The wall opposite the sergeant's desk is filled with most-wanted posters, signs warning people to keep an eye out for pickpockets and unattended packages and suspicious activity, and tips for being safe in the city: "Guard Your Personal Belongings at All Times" and "Stay Alert."

To the left of the sergeant's desk is a window into an office where a group of policemen mill about, waiting for something to happen. Farther back into the precinct, I see other officers walking around, ducking in and out of offices—the same kind of offices that the policewoman dragged me into and handed me Mike's note.

The waiting area is filled with people who have come to file complaints about neighbors or family members or stolen property or landlords or merchants or urban bureaucracy.

A family of tourists with blonde hair, pale skin, and light-colored eyes are gathered at the far end of the desk talking to an officer. The father is trying to explain that something has happened to them. Their English is bad and the officer tries to guess their complaint: a stolen purse or a theater ticket scam or an assault. Each time the officer makes a guess, the father shakes his head no.

"Anybody speak . . . I don't know . . . Swedish," the police officer yells back into the precinct.

Next to the Scandinavian family, a short Latina stands on her tiptoes and speaks Spanish to another officer. A group of black teenagers is sitting in a row of chairs along the far wall. They have their arms crossed and their legs splayed as if they're prepared to sit there all day to get whatever it is they've come for.

I take all of this in, hoping that the place itself will jar memory loose. I take a deep breath and exhale it forcefully.

"What are you here for?" the desk sergeant asks. I turn and look up at him. He has a thick body, a pockmarked face, and thin graying hair.

"Well?" he says from his perch.

"I need a police report," I manage to say, sounding unsure of myself.

"You need to file one?" he asks.

"No," I say, "I need to get a copy of one."

The desk sergeant calls over to another officer, who beckons me to one of the swing gates.

"What are you here for?" the second officer asks me. He's a young guy in his early thirties with reddish-brown hair—the same shade that Mike had when he was alive. His skin, too, is ruddy the way Mike's was. His appearance takes me aback.

For a moment, I think about telling the officer the story I've been telling people for decades about how Mike died and how my family reacted—especially my father. But standing in that precinct house, I suddenly realize that my story about Mike is no different than any other story this police officer—or any other police officer anywhere—has heard a thousand times. It may well be the same kind of story the Scandinavian family and the Latina are telling, and perhaps the same one the teenagers are waiting to tell.

I think about turning around and walking out of the precinct, telling my shrink later that the details don't matter. Perhaps, I tell myself, the details will just make Mike's death seem ordinary and inconsequential. But then I think that this is my shrink's point.

"So?" the officer asks. He grabs the top of the swing gate and leans a little closer to me.

"A police report," I say.

I try to determine the color of the officer's eyes to see if they are green like Mike's were. But the officer has puffy eyes and I can't tell.

"When did the incident occur?" the officer asks me, leaning back and grabbing a form off the desk.

"1993," I say.

"1993," he says, dropping the form. "That's a long time ago."

I look over at the Scandinavian family to see how they're progressing. The father is still trying to communicate his complaint to the officer, while the rest of the family has retreated to seats next to the disgruntled teenagers.

"I know," I say. "But still, I want the report."

The officer shrugs his shoulders and tells me to wait while he consults his superiors. He walks into the office with the window.

I lightly tap the bottom of the swing gate with my shoe.

I see the officer explaining my request to the men inside the office. A few of the men shake their heads. A few look at me as if I'm pitiful. They discuss the options for a minute or two and then the red-headed officer returns.

"You have to go downtown," he says, rubbing his chest as if he has heartburn. "The incident is too old. You have to make a request to have the report retrieved."

He tells me the address—100 Police Plaza—just across from City Hall and behind the Borough of Manhattan Municipal Building near the Brooklyn Bridge.

I thank him and then head out the door.

The New York City Police Headquarters looks like a fortress with thick brown-brick walls and rows of small windows and a guard-house out front.

I approach the guardhouse and begin to tell the officer inside what I'm there for. He's not interested in what I have to say. Instead, he points to a side building where the visitors entrance is located. I walk over, stand in a short line where visitors go through a security checkpoint, and wait my turn.

"What are you here for?" a tall officer asks me.

"An old report" I say.

"FOI," the officer calls over to a second officer on the other side of the X-ray scanner.

"FOI?" I ask.

"Freedom of Information," he says.

I put my keys and cellphone and loose change in a tray and walk through the metal detector. I pick up my personal items on the other side. The officer points me to the front entrance of the fortress-like building.

Inside, I stop at yet another desk.

"What are you here for?" an officer asks.

I think the question, "What are you here for?" must be a part of every police officer's training, a way to make it sound as if they care but without actually caring. When I hear the question for the fourth time, I feel numb, like I've been walking around inside of a maze and no longer care if I find the exit.

"FOI," I say simply, as if Mike's death has been reduced to this acronym.

The officer asks me to look into a small camera on his desk; he snaps my picture, prints a visitor's badge, and points me down the hall were the Freedom of Information office is located.

There, a woman looks at me kindly, as if she's had a bad day and something about my face tells her that I'm not going to give her a hard time.

"What can I do for you, honey?" she asks. She's not wearing a police uniform, but rather a beige blouse and a denim skirt. Her hair is piled high on top of her head.

"FOI," I say, as if I'm a researcher who has been through this routine a hundred times.

"Yes," she says. "But what kind of information do you need?" She takes a pen from her desk, ready to write down what I have to say.

Cautiously, I tell her the bare facts of Mike's case. She looks at me and nods her head. She asks me for more details—the same way my shrink had—and I give her a few. I know that she's asking me for details so that she can narrow the search for Mike's files. But still, I feel as if she cares, or at least as if she understands that what I need is more than just facts, but rather a way to find comfort.

When I finish, she reaches over and places her hand on top of my forearm the way my mother might.

"We'll see what we can get for you," she says. "But I can't promise you anything."

I thank her and retrace my steps out of Police Headquarters.

A few weeks later, I receive the police report. As I'm flipping through the mail, the official blue seal of the City of New York on the envelope jumps out at me. I sit down at the dining room table in my apartment and open the envelope. I take out the sheets of paper, which have been so badly copied that the numbered boxes that ask for the time and the date and the place of the incident are blurry and hard to read. I rub my finger over the box that gives the date of the incident, trying to clear away some of the blurry print and read it more clearly.

I notice immediately that at the top of the report, it reads "Complaint," as if Mike's death was a kind of annoyance that someone called in as they might if neighbors were playing their music too loud, or if a car alarm wouldn't shut off.

The complaint says upfront that the officers are there to "Investigate D.O.A." It gives the address where Mike lived in the city: 67 E. Eleventh Street, Apt. No. 723; and the address where he died: 1605 Broadway, Suite 2906. It lists the contents of his personal effects that were found in the hotel where he died, the same effects the police officer handed to my mother in the plastic bag, and which my mother held to her chest: brown leather wallet, red leather address book, triathlon watch.

In a large box on the form that asks the presiding officer to "Reconstruct Occurrence including Method of Entry & Escape— include Unique or Unusual Actions," the officer typed:

Victim checked into hotel 10/26/1993 and was to check out on 10/28/1993 at 1200 hours. Hotel employees attempted to enter suite 2906 w/ master key but could not enter room because chain lock was engaged. Hotel security then broke chain lock and opened door discovering victim lying face up with only his undergarments next to a small desk. Pronounced by EMS#4206 at 1512 hrs.

I'd known that Mike died in a hotel room in Times Square. I hadn't known that he'd checked in two days before they found him, or that he'd chain locked the door. Did he expect someone to come along and try to get into the room before he could complete the act of dying? A friend, perhaps, or a brother who had come to rescue him? I didn't know that he was found lying on the floor face up—I assumed he had died lying in the hotel bed as if he'd fallen asleep but didn't wake up. I didn't know that he died in his underwear as if he hadn't thought about how he'd be found, how embarrassing it might be to be found dead in "only his undergarments."

Perhaps, he hadn't really meant to die. Perhaps, he'd checked into the hotel and only planned to play at dying, to give himself a couple of days to see what it might be like to die but not go through with it. To get ready for bed, to take the drug, but to expect he'd wake up after a day or two, and then go on with his life. The same way I had when I was a teenager and took a handful of sleeping pills, expecting to die but waking up the next morning instead.

Farther down on the form, in a box marked "Details," the officer writes, "The family was notified. At 1900 hours . . . received a phone call from the father . . . I supplied him with the proper instructions to claim his son's body for burial."

I hadn't known that my father talked with the detective who found Mike's body. What had my father asked the detective, I wonder? Had he asked what had happened and why? Had my father picked up the phone, heard the detective's voice, and cried out "My son. My son!" Was his grief too much for him to bear? Did my father weep? Did he grow angry and blame the city for his son's death? Did he blame God? Did my father ask the detective if he was certain it was Mike? Did my father try to challenge the detective in an attempt to believe that Mike wasn't dead but still alive, still back in his apartment or at his office downtown? Did he refuse to listen to the detective?

More likely, my father called just to get the details on how to claim Mike's body, the forms necessary to fill out, the steps he needed to take. I am sure he listened calmly and patiently. Then, my father would have thanked the detective for his time before hanging up the phone. He would treat it as a routine business transaction, like a failed asset that one of his clients had written off as a business expense.

My father has never spoken to me about that phone call. He didn't say a word to me about it that day in 1993 when we walked out of the medical examiner's office and headed to the 18th Precinct. Nor has he mentioned it in the two decades since Mike has been dead. I've never heard my father say Mike's name out loud from that day to the present.

In the same envelope as the original complaint, there is a follow-up complaint. It reads in part, "On this day at 0815 I called the M.E.'s office and spoke with Det. Carbone. He informs me that the body was released to the family for burial, cause of death was overdose."

My father took Mike's body back to Indianapolis, the hometown Mike and I had abandoned long before, vowing never to return. In preparing for his suicide, Mike failed to leave behind instructions on what should be done with his body or his property. Even though he was a lawyer, Mike failed to draw up a will, so that, in the end, my father did get all of Mike's money and all of his other assets worth a few hundred thousand dollars.

My father never comes to visit me in New York. He believes the city is the Sodom and Gomorrah of the East. He believes it is an evil city that infects everyone with its moral decay and unspeakable diseases. I don't think my father was surprised that Mike killed himself. In my father's eyes, it was the price that had to be paid for such a sin.

I put the complaint back in its envelope. I put the envelope in a bowl on the dining room table where we keep old mail that needs to be sorted through to either throw out or respond to. It will stay there for weeks, so that when I pass through the kitchen the official blue seal on the envelope reminds me that sooner or later I have to deal with it.

The Letter

From my second-floor bedroom in the blue house on Caroline Street in Washington, D.C., I had a clear view out the window to the magnolia tree in the backyard. I'd never seen a magnolia tree before moving here in 1989. Watching it bloom that spring made me feel as if I lived in some exotic American city like Savannah or New Orleans where, I imagined, magnolia trees bloomed in abundance.

Before moving to D.C., my mother objected to my leaving Indianapolis. She said D.C. was a violent town and that I'd be dead from a gunshot wound within the first month. She'd say anything to keep her children close to her. She lived for Sunday dinners surrounded by family at the table we'd eaten at since we were kids. It was a long table made of soft pine that accumulated the scratches and indents and stains from decades of use.

I wasn't the first one to move away from home. Mike had left in 1985. After graduating from law school, he took a job at Morgan Stanley in New York. But Mike had always been expected to leave home—he was smart and ambitious—while my family assumed that I would stay in Indianapolis, get an accounting job, marry, and have kids of my own like the rest of my brothers. I didn't seem adventurous or daring enough to move away and become someone my family would consider exotic, like a writer.

I had a roommate in the blue house on Caroline Street. His name was Jimmy. He was tall and thin with a sharp nose and a weak chin. Jimmy had the larger of the two bedrooms, facing the front of the house where a white picket fence ran along the small bit of lawn separating the front of the house from the sidewalk.

I'd met Jimmy through a mutual friend, who thought we'd make good roommates because Jimmy was outgoing and I seemed shy. Jimmy was an architect and worked out of the house. I sold men's shoes at Nordstrom in the Pentagon City Mall in Arlington, Virginia.

Jimmy and I had a ritual: on Saturday mornings we'd sit on the couch watching *Pee-wee's Playhouse* on TV while eating pancakes and drinking coffee. In my family, we had no rituals, except those dictated by the church and our pious father: saying grace before meals, going to Mass every Sunday, kneeling by our beds to say a prayer before going to sleep.

The Saturday in the middle of that summer when I received the phone call, I walked downstairs to make pancakes and brew coffee. Jimmy's bedroom door was still shut.

I was wearing a tight-fitting red tank top and a pair of gray cotton gym shorts that were a size too small. Around my six brothers, I only ever wore oversized T-shirts and baggy pants, afraid that my thin body looked vulnerable, and that my three older brothers would want to hurt me.

Once, when I was around nine years old, my younger brother Eddy invited his friends over to our house for a slumber party. They slept in sleeping bags lined up in a row on the floor in the bedroom I shared with Eddy. Our bedroom looked like a camping site that a troop of Boy Scouts had taken over.

When it was bedtime, I went into the bathroom and changed into my pajamas. The other boys stayed in the room and stripped down to their underwear. When I returned, the lights were out. I thought, at first, that they'd already gone to sleep, but I was wrong. Instead, they were leaping from Eddy's bed to mine in their underwear. One of Eddy's friends had a flashlight and was shining it on their bodies, as if the boys were so many Tarzans swinging through the jungle in the moonlight.

I was nervous watching them. I'd always felt uncomfortable around other boys because I wanted to look at their bodies. I knew from my oldest brother Tony, however, that boys who liked to look at other boys were perverts that deserved to be punished: to be punched and kicked and stomped on.

By the time the pancakes were made and the coffee was brewed, I thought Jimmy would've made it downstairs. I took my plate and mug into the front room and turned on the TV.

I'd just shoved too much food into my mouth when I heard footsteps behind me coming down the carpeted stairs.

"About time, sleepyhead," I said through a mouthful of pancake. Then, I turned around, but instead of Jimmy, there was a guy my age standing in his underwear on the last step. He was tall with pale skin and thinning blond hair.

"Hello," he said.

My cheeks were swollen with food.

He grinned.

Embarrassed, I swung around on the couch to hide my face. The plate on my lap tilted and spilled syrup on my thigh.

"Shit," I said, setting the plate on the side table and wiping up the syrup with a paper towel.

When I finished cleaning up my mess, I turned back to see the cute guy in his underwear walk into the kitchen. He opened and closed kitchen cabinets until he found a glass, and then he filled it with water from the tap.

He walked back toward me with his glass of water. I didn't turn away. I stared at his smooth chest and his flat stomach. I let my eyes drift down to his crotch and saw that unmistakable dot-of-a-stain in the pouch of his underwear. He smiled as I stared at him.

"Bye," he said as he passed me and went back up the stairs.

I'd known Jimmy for a couple of months before we moved in together, but I didn't realize he slept with so many guys.

When I was twelve, I wanted to do more than stare at other boys. I wanted to kiss them, and caress their chests in the way I'd seen my oldest brother Tony kiss and stroke girls on the living room couch when our parents were out. But I also knew that if Tony ever caught me, he would hang me upside down from my second floor bedroom window and threaten to drop me onto the paved driveway below.

I didn't know then that Mike was also gay. I've often wondered how my life would've been different had I known that I had a gay brother.

I was a lonely kid growing up. I felt different from my brothers and worried that my difference put me in danger. So, I kept quiet. I stayed in the background, where I thought I'd be safe.

One day when I was sitting alone on our front porch, a boy Mike's age rode his bike up to me. He asked if I'd like to play a game in his basement. He had curly blond hair and blue eyes and broad shoulders. I'd seen him at the swim pool we belonged to. He hung out with a group of public school kids that our mother warned us to stay away from. Public school kids, my mother said, were always looking to get into trouble. The boy's name was Craig.

I followed Craig to his house. He took me down into his basement to play pool, and to show me his baseball collection. Once we were down there, he asked if I'd like to see him naked. I didn't say no. He took off his clothes and stroked his cock. He asked me to lick it. I did.

On my way back home, I tried to get the taste of him out of my mouth—a metallic taste as if I'd run my tongue over the top of a battery. I continually spit onto the side of the road. When I got home, I brushed my teeth until my gums hurt, and scraped the toothbrush over my tongue.

That summer, I returned to Craig's basement a half dozen times. Each time, we spent a few minutes playing pool and looking at his baseball cards. Then he'd take his shirt off. He had smooth skin and tufts of soft hair under his arms and a thin waist. He'd lie down on the carpeted floor of the basement, and wiggle out of his shorts and his underwear. His cock was erect. I knelt down and gave him a blowjob. A few times, I tried caressing his stomach, but he didn't want me to touch him. He moved my hands off of his body. After each encounter, I walked home and tried to get the taste of him out of my mouth.

A few minutes after the first guy came down the stairs in the house on Caroline Street, a second one descended in his underwear. He, too, stopped on the bottom step. I turned away from watching *Pee-wee's Playhouse* to look at this second guy. He had straight black hair and a belly that protruded ever so slightly.

"Hi," he said, scratching the hair on his chest.

I waved without saying a word. He smiled, turned away from me and headed toward the kitchen. As he passed me, I caught the last remnants of Grey Flannel cologne coming off his body.

He too opened and closed kitchen cabinets until he found a glass. The sound of the cabinets smacking against their frames reminded me of my brothers storming through my mother's kitchen, raiding the cabinets for food while she begged them to take it easy. Periodically, the hinges and the pulls on my mother's cabinets would come loose and she'd take out a screwdriver from the drawer to tighten them.

The dark-haired guy filled his glass with water, and walked back toward me while I kept my eyes on his body. I grinned. He said goodbye and padded up the stairs with that faint smell of cologne trailing behind him.

By the time I was sixteeen—and Mike was off at college—I'd sneak out of the house in the middle of the night to meet older men who sat in idling station wagons in the parking lot of the local elementary school. They'd open their passenger-side doors and let me in. I'd suck them off, then they'd shove me out of their cars and race back home. During the day, I'd cruise the mall and became an expert at using storefront windows as mirrors to watch other men staring into other storefront windows. Occasionally, they'd follow me into the mall's restroom where I knelt on the dirty tile floor of a toilet stall and let them push my head into their laps.

At home, I became vigilant, watching my family at the dinner table to see if they registered a change in me. I stood for hours in front of the bathroom mirror and practiced emptying my face until I became expressionless. I learned to watch more clearly out of my peripheral vision so that I would never be blindsided by fag-bashers or the police who were always on the lookout for boys like me. I taught myself to gaze without appearing to gaze. I became an expert at keeping secrets, of diverting attention away from myself, of hiding in plain sight. I was an innocent-looking teenage pervert.

I turned back to the TV as Tito the Lifeguard sauntered into the playhouse in his red Hawaiian-print bathing suit. His tanned body and big biceps and muscular legs were the reason I liked watching *Pee-wee's Playhouse.* Every gay man I knew watched *Pee-wee's Playhouse,* a show so filled with gay jokes that it seemed more a gay burlesque than a Saturday morning kid's show. From Pee-wee's overly rouged cheeks to Miss Yvonne's bouffant hair to Jamby the Genie's campy delivery of one-liners and Chairy begging, "Come over here and sit on me, Pee-wee," the *Playhouse* was the gayest thing on TV.

Finally, Jimmy walked downstairs in a sheer T-shirt and pale blue boxer shorts.

"Tito is so fucking hot," he said, walking into the kitchen to grab a mug and fill it with coffee.

"Busy night," I commented.

"They're cute, aren't they?" he asked, plopping down on the couch next to me.

Jimmy smelled of Gray Flannel cologne and salt water and the mustiness of sex.

"They're very cute," I said.

"They're boyfriends," he said, covering his mouth to prevent himself from laughing out loud in his trademark high-pitched scream-of-a-laugh.

Jimmy sipped his coffee and reached over to run his index finger through a pool of syrup on my plate, something one of my brothers might have done. With Jimmy, though, I didn't mind because I liked him.

When I moved to D.C. in my mid-twenties, I had a difficult time adjusting. In Indianapolis, I taught myself to keep my sexuality a secret, to appear one way in public—fragile and uncertain—and another in dark places—greedy and assertive.

Jimmy confused me because he was so open about his sexuality. We'd walk down Sixteenth Street in the middle of the day and he thought nothing of saying hello to a cute guy who was stopped at a crosswalk with us, while I pretended not to even notice him. Jimmy would casually walk into a video store and browse gay porn while I pretended to be interested in romantic comedies. Jimmy was always bringing guys home, parading them around the house. Once when I'd brought a guy home and Jimmy caught me sneaking him out of the house in the middle of the night, I apologized so profusely that Jimmy laughed, saying, "I'm not your mother, you know."

One time, when I was in my early twenties and still living in Indianapolis, Mike came home for a visit—he'd moved to New York by then and was working at Morgan Stanley. I'd had an argument with my mother about picking him up at the airport: she'd wanted to come along but I was insistent that I go alone. I'd figured out by then that Mike was gay—he lived in the Village, spent his summer weekends out in the Pines on Fire Island, and only ever talked about the men he hung out with. I assumed that he'd figured out that I was gay, too. I wanted the time between the airport and home to be something special between us. I thought we might be able to recalibrate our relationship so that we could talk frankly about being gay and about our early sexual encounters—I was willing to confess to mine if he was willing to do the same—about the men we dated and those we wanted to date, about the codes by which I imagined gay men lived. I wanted Mike to be the older gay brother who'd teach me how to be gay, how to live openly. I wanted him to teach me how men fucked other men, something I hadn't done yet. I was afraid that I'd get it wrong and embarrass myself.

I wanted to tell Mike that for as long as I could remember I wanted to be a writer, and I wanted him to be proud of me for having this dream. A dream none of my other brothers or my sister would understand. They were too provincial, I thought, while Mike was a sophisticated urbanite who must have had dozens of friends who were writers and artists and performers.

I wore a tight red-and-white-striped shirt and button-fly Levis to the airport. I was young and slim, and I liked my body. When Mike got off the plane and saw me standing at the gate waiting for him—bouncing from one foot to the next like an excited child—he smiled.

"Did you wear that for me?" he asked, looking me up and down.

Mike was holding a black leather overnight bag. He wore penny loafers and creased jeans and a button-down shirt he'd bought at Barney's or Brooks Brothers or one of those other high-end stores that no one else in our family ever shopped.

I blushed and pulled at my shirt as if it were suffocating me.

"They're just clothes," I said.

"Uh huh," he said, still smiling.

We walked through the terminal without saying a word to each other. When we got into the car, he asked how the family was, and I said they were fine. I asked him how New York was treating him, and he said it was okay.

We didn't talk about being gay—or about my dream of being a writer. We didn't open up to each other about our sexual secrets. We didn't even attempt to joke about being queer boys in an aggressively heterosexual family—two pansies in a field of thistles. We never even said the word "gay" to each other—not then and not in the years that followed. As children, the word had been over-laden with hate and disgust; it was the word my youngest brother Pat shouted when he was angry and vengeful, the word my oldest brother Tony used when he turned mean and threatening. The word itself was hardwired into our brains like a bomb wrapped around our central cortex. Mike and I were afraid, I think, that if we said the word "gay" our heads would explode. Now, I wonder what would've happened if we were able to say that word to each other. Perhaps it would've allowed Mike and me to be more honest and intimate with each other. Perhaps it would've allowed us to help each other unlearn the harmful lessons we'd learned from having grown up in our family.

Mike and I were men who liked to have sex with other men. We were men who would never marry a woman and have children; the only kind of men our conservative hometown seemed to value. We were sons who violated the tenets of our father and his faith. We were brothers, even, but we were never gay brothers.

When I moved to D.C., Mike told me to find an apartment in DuPont Circle, but without telling me why—it was the gay neighborhood in D.C., which I learned only when I moved there. It was the only advice Mike ever gave me, and I was grateful for it.

Watching *Pee-wee's Playhouse* back at the house on Caroline Street in D.C. with Jimmy sitting next to me, I felt as if I were beginning to form a new kind of family than the one I'd left in Indianapolis. A family of gay friends where Jimmy was the only sibling I needed, the only gay brother that cared for me.

I didn't know it when I lived in D.C., but I found out after he died that Mike was doing something similar in New York. At his funeral, Mike's friends and colleagues were surprised to learn that Mike had so many siblings and that he grew up in a middle-class family in the Midwest. Living in New York, Mike had fashioned a completely new life for himself with a completely new family history. Mike told people in New York that he was an only child, whose parents had died when Mike was young. He had a modest trust fund that necessitated he work, he told people, but which also allowed him to jet off to the South of France whenever the mood struck him.

"I think Cowboy Curtis is sexier," Jimmy said. "He's got big feet."

"You know what they say about men with big feet?" I said.

"Big cocks," Jimmy said.

"That's not how the joke goes."

"I know," he said. "But still . . ."

I hated talking openly about sex, even with Jimmy with whom I felt close. My early sexual experiences made me guarded and defensive. I thought that I was the only boy in the world who'd had sex when I was young, and that these sexual encounters had somehow tainted me. I thought I was untouchable. I was a boy who knew how to please a man—especially if he were a stranger—and a boy who liked doing so. I believed that if anyone found this out—especially people I loved, like Jimmy—they would turn their backs on me.

"Time to take a shower," Jimmy said as he got up from the couch and headed for the stairs. "We'll try not to be too loud . . ."

"Yeah, right," I said, turning back to the TV.

I stared up at the ceiling as I listened to Jimmy walk into his bedroom, and then the three of them walk into the bathroom. I heard the water in the shower turn on. I turned up the volume on the TV so I wouldn't have to hear them.

Then, the phone rang.

We had a wall-mounted phone in the kitchen and another phone in Jimmy's office. When the phone rang in our house, it was almost always for Jimmy.

I lazily walked into the kitchen, carrying my coffee mug. Out the kitchen window I could see the magnolia tree, which had long since lost its waxy flowers.

"He's in the shower," I said as soon as I picked up the receiver.

"Who's in the shower?" the voice on the other end of the phone asked.

It took me a few seconds to realize that it was my mother calling. We didn't talk that often, and when we did, I was the one who called her—it was expected of me. She never called unless there was an emergency.

"What's wrong?" I asked her.

"Who's in the shower?" she asked again.

"No one," I said, fidgeting with the long cord. "My roommate," I corrected myself. "Jimmy."

I hadn't come out to my family, and being in the closet made me paranoid. When I moved in with Jimmy, I thought that my mother would easily intuit that I was gay. Even though Jimmy and I weren't lovers, and even though plenty of straight men lived with male roommates. Still, I often overexplained my living arrangements to my mother, carefully giving her the layout of the house and emphasizing our separate bedrooms.

"I see," my mother said.

"Is everything all right?" I asked her.

"What's with this letter?" my mother asked.

My stomach tensed. I thought that maybe she'd gotten a collection notice for my student loans that were past due. We were a family that took their financial obligations seriously, as if debt were the first sign of moral decay.

"What letter?" I asked, topping off my mug of coffee.

"Your brother Michael wrote a letter," she told me.

"Okay," I said, relieved that I wasn't the one on the hook. I didn't understand, however, why Mike would send a letter to my mother. We weren't a family that sent letters to one another.

The sound from the TV was loud. Embarrassed that my mother might hear what I was watching, I opened the door to the back porch and stepped outside. I set my coffee on the porch railing.

"Why don't you call him and find out?" I asked my mother.

"He's on vacation," she said.

Even though he didn't have a trust fund, Mike did have money that allowed him to vacation in the South of France when work permitted it. Although looking back, I wonder if Mike ever jetted off anywhere or simply told people that he did. Maybe it was all part of the fantasy life he was creating in New York. Instead of going to the South of France, perhaps he hid out in the city for a few weeks—or went down to the Jersey shore.

There was an alley behind the house that served the houses on Caroline Street and on the next street over. The backs of our houses were close enough so that we could see into each other's windows.

I was always afraid that someone was spying on me. Standing on the porch talking with my mother on the phone, I tried to keep my voice down.

"What's in the letter?" I asked.

Even though Mike and I had our sexuality in common, I didn't trust him. I never trusted him. He was too concerned with his own self-interests to care whether or not he hurt others.

Once, assuming greater intimacy than existed, I told Mike in confidence that our younger brother Rob was having trouble in his marriage—my mother had confided this to me. Mike immediately phoned Rob and told him that it was all right to get a divorce. He said that even though no one in our family ever got divorced, it was okay for him to be the first.

"Marriage is a silly convention," Mike had said to Rob. "Nobody really needs to get married."

Rob was angry with Mike, of course, and complained to my mother that she'd broken his confidence. My mother, in turn, called me and chided me for abusing her trust. Then I yelled at Mike for spreading gossip.

Now, I took a sip of coffee and waited.

My mother didn't speak for a few seconds. She sighed.

Mike and I had come to a tacit agreement: our lives in New York and D.C. were none of our family's business. When Mike and I went to Studio 54—where men waving giant dildos danced half-naked on speakers—I was never to hint to my mother that I'd even gone to see Mike, let alone that he'd taken me to such a notorious sex den. Or when he came to D.C—and he came to visit me only once—and we stood at the bar at JRs and he pointed out men he thought were my type—even though he had no idea what my type was—he would never relay back home that he thought I liked men who wore suspenders and slim-legged pants.

Even in these trips to clubs and bars, Mike and I never talked the way I imagined gay brothers would talk. Instead, I felt as if he was trying to shock me, to test my sexual limits so that he could judge whether or not I was more adventurous than he was, or more reserved. It was as if to Mike, our being gay brothers was a competition he was determined to win.

"He says a lot of things in the letter," my mother finally said.

"Like what?" I asked.

"Well," she said hesitantly.

I imagined my mother on the phone in her kitchen, sitting at the yellow Formica counter where I used to eat lunch when I was a kid. I imagined her fidgeting with one of the plastic apples that sat in a wicker basket on the counter along with fake oranges and plums, the way she used to do when she was talking with one of her girlfriends. I imagined that my father was nowhere in earshot; he was probably back in his den watching a golf tournament. I imagined that Mike's letter lay beside my mother on the counter.

If Mike and I had an implied understanding that we'd keep our private lives from our family, I assumed this meant that we would never come out to them.

Listening to my mother fiddle on the other end of the line, however, I suddenly understood the content of Mike's letter. He had come out to my parents, and I was irritated with him. At the very least, he could've told me first so that I could have prepared for this phone call.

I grew fidgety, drumming my fingers on the side of my leg. If my mother knew that Mike was gay, it wouldn't be difficult for her to figure out that I was gay too. Mike and I were too much alike—the same mannerisms and expressions; the same lifestyle. We were her only sons who lived away from Indianapolis, the only ones who didn't bring girlfriends home for the holidays or talk endlessly about raising a family.

It was classic Mike to drop a bomb and then walk away, leaving the mess for someone else to clean up. He did this nearly every time he came home on his short visits. Announcing on his last day of winter break when he was in college, for example, that he no longer believed in God and that he thought our father's devotion to the church was juvenile. Or how, when he came back for one

Memorial Day weekend and my family was sitting on the back patio drinking beer and listening to the Indy 500 on the radio, he starting railing against President Reagan, who my father—and almost everyone else in my family—had voted for and idolized. As the blood in my father's face crept up his neck, the rest of us slipped away.

"I just want you to know," my mother said. She sounded as if she were holding back tears. "All I've ever wanted for my children is that they be happy."

"I know that," I said to her softly.

The temperature was warm even in the shade of the magnolia tree. My tank top was suffocating.

"And I'm not so blind," she said in the aggressive way my mother had learned by dealing with a household of boys who constantly tried to pull the wool over her eyes: to sneak out past curfew, to try and get out of doing chores, to talk back.

"I know," I said again.

In that moment when my mother seemed to be reaching out to me, to bridge the gap that had grown between us since I moved away from Indianapolis, perhaps I should've come out to her myself. Perhaps, I should've tried to explain that I had to leave home. That to me, Indianapolis represented all the pain and loneliness I felt growing up. But I didn't say anything because I was afraid that I would hurt her, and I didn't want to hurt her.

There was a glass panel in the top half of the back door. I could see that Jimmy and his dates had come downstairs and were lounging on the couch watching TV, their limbs intertwined. They looked like spent satyrs, too happy and too sated to care about anything.

"I'm disappointed," my mother went on, her tone softening. "Of all my children, I would've expected *you* to come talk to me about this . . ."

My mother and I had been close when I was a child. She saw that I was a sensitive boy and that my brothers were not always kind to me. She tried to protect me. Once, my brothers stormed into the house after playing outside and ran into the living room where I'd been listening to the soundtrack of *The Sound of Music* on the hi-fi. They caterwauled and drowned out Julie Andrews. I screamed for them to stop, which only encouraged more teasing. My mother had shooed them out of the room. I was boiling mad, but she came over and stroked my hair and tried to calm me.

I was her special boy, and my brothers knew this, which made living with them even more difficult. They teased me relentlessly, calling me a sissy and a fag and a momma's boy. When I grew older, I blamed my mother for coddling me, for making me weak and vulnerable. When I finally left home, I held her at arm's length as I tried to shield myself from the cruelties of others.

If Mike and I couldn't use the word "gay" with each other, I was certain my mother would never ask me if I was gay. Even if she suspected that this was true—How could she not? I took solace in knowing this.

"It's my fault, isn't it?" my mother asked me. She was crying; her voice came over the phone in short gasps.

"It's not your fault," I said, patting my chest to keep my voice calm. "It's nobody's fault."

Inside the house, Jimmy and his dates untwined their limbs and stretched. I thought they might be heading out to grab brunch. I was eager to get off the phone and ask if I could join them, even though I'd already eaten.

Over the phone, I heard my mother blow her nose. I grabbed the door handle, ready to go inside and hang up the phone.

"At the end of the letter," my mother whispered as if she didn't want anyone else to hear, "your brother wrote, 'P.S. Andy is too.'"

For a second, I didn't understand the implication of Mike's postscript. I had no context for understanding what he was making light of since I'd never seen this letter—nor have I seen it since. At first, I didn't want to believe that Mike had outed me. Then, I knew that he had.

"He did what!" I yelled without meaning to yell. Jimmy and his dates turned and looked at me. I imagined that my neighbors eating their breakfasts also heard me. I ducked down on the porch.

My heart beat fast, and my pulse throbbed behind my eyes. It felt as if time was racing past me and I was stuck in some strange and unknowable place.

I took a deep breath to calm myself. I opened my eyes. I reached out and grabbed the porch railing to anchor me. My body began to shake. Mike had no right to out me in a letter, I said to myself. He timed it perfectly, of course. He'd sent the letter and then gone on vacation, knowing that my mother would call me for an explanation.

"It's all right," my mother said in a soothing voice, the one she used when I was a boy and lying sick in bed.

"Who read this?" I demanded. I stood up and started to walk down the steps of the porch. I wanted to get away from the house. The phone cord reached its limit at the bottom step.

"Everyone," my mother said gently.

"What do you mean 'everyone'?" I asked, tugging at the phone cord.

"Mike photocopied the letter," my mother said, "and sent one to each of your siblings."

"Goddamn it," I yelled, yanking at the phone cord more forcefully.

"Andrew!" my mother scolded me.

I lowered myself down on the step. I was too angry to say anything.

"Your brothers came over to the house when they got the letter," my mother said. "Eddy was in tears."

I flashed back to that moment Eddy's friends had slept over at our house and played Tarzan in our bedroom.

"I have to go," I said suddenly. I didn't want to hear how my siblings had reacted to Mike's letter. I especially didn't want to hear how my father reacted. I imagined he immediately dismissed the idea, thinking that it was impossible for him to have one gay son, much less two. I imagined that after reading the letter, he went back into his den, sat down at his desk, and busied himself paying bills or balancing his checkbook.

Back in the house, I hung up the phone, and then ran upstairs, ignoring Jimmy's attempt to see if I was okay. Slamming my bedroom door, I sat down on my bed. I felt the shadows of my childhood descend on me like a toxic cloud. I could never go back and visit my family, I thought. I could never talk to them again. I would be too ashamed, too defenseless.

In the week that followed, I heard from my sister Marie, who said that she'd known all along. She said that when we were kids and I preferred playing with her instead of my brothers, she thought of me more as a sister than her brother. She said that in high school it was pretty obvious because I never acted like the other boys: I wasn't aggressive toward girls, and I didn't ogle them as they walked the hallways. Marie sounded proud to have her suspicions confirmed. I was annoyed at her smugness. I also heard from my younger brother Rob, who liked to think of himself as unflappable. He said he'd known tons of guys who were gay. He said it wasn't a big deal.

I never heard from my other brothers—Tony, Joe, Eddy, Pat—all of who seemed to want to forget the whole thing.

When he got back from vacation, Mike called me.

I took the call in the kitchen. I stood looking out the window. It was early in the evening. Across the alley, lights came on in the kitchens of our neighbors. Jimmy was out at the bars on Sixteenth Street.

"How'd it go?" Mike asked as if he were asking about a date I'd been on.

"You're fucking kidding me," I said loudly.

On the kitchen windowsill we kept a small glass jelly jar in which Jimmy placed herbs and wild flowers. When the magnolia tree bloomed, he'd snip off a flower and put it in the jelly jar. The fragrance from that one flower filled the house.

I reached over to the jelly jar. Jimmy had put a sprig of lilac in it. I rubbed one of the petals between my fingers. I remembered the lilacs that grew beneath my mother's bedroom window when I was a boy.

"I know. I know," Mike said.

Despite the soothing smell on my fingers, I couldn't stop my hands from shaking.

I'd been expecting Mike's phone call ever since I'd talked with my mother a few weeks earlier. I'd spent sleepless nights planning out what I'd say to him. I was getting ready to launch into a diatribe about the ethics of outing. I was going to force him to admit that he'd done irreparable damage to my psyche. I was going to get some kind of concession out of him as if I were the lawyer in the family. In the end, though, I just broke down and cried over the phone while he listened.

I leaned forward and rested my head on the overhead cabinets. I put my palms flat on the counter and let all of the anger and frustration and anxiety that'd been building up inside of me rush out.

Mike was quiet until I calmed down. I tore a sheet of paper towel from the wooden holder we kept on the counter and blew my nose.

"It's for the best," Mike said. "No more hiding. At least not from them."

I nodded even though Mike obviously couldn't see me. I threw the paper towel into the trash bin beneath the sink

"Eddy cried," I said.

"What an idiot," Mike said.

I walked over to the back door and stepped out onto the porch. From one of our neighbor's open windows, Madonna's song "Like a Prayer" floated out into the warm night.

"Don't ever do that again," I said to Mike.

"It's already done," he said.

"You know what I mean."

"Okay," he said.

We talked for a few more minutes. He told me about his vacation. He'd gone to Capri. It'd been fun, he said. The sea was amazing and the food was incredible and the boys . . . well, Mike demurred . . . the boys were fun.

Through the window in the back door, I saw Jimmy come into the house and run upstairs. He'd come home to change clothes for a long night out at the clubs.

I told Mike that we'd see each other soon, said goodbye, came back into the house, and hung up the phone.

I went into the front room, turned on the TV, sat down on the couch, and listened to Jimmy rushing around his bedroom above me.

Salient Facts

My husband David and I have a house in upstate New York. It's a one-bedroom gambrel house set in the middle of seven acres of wooded land. We bought the house in 2007 and have been coming up here every weekend for nearly a decade.

In between two books on a shelf in the loft of our upstate house, I keep a document titled "The Salient Facts of Patient Michael J. Barnes." Mike wrote it a year before he died. I found the document in a filing cabinet in Mike's apartment when I flew to New York to identify his body at the morgue in Midtown. The document details the period in Mike's life from early 1991 until late in 1992 when, he writes, "I am unable to sleep because of anxiety & fear over HIV + diagnosis."

Periodically, I pull the papers down off the shelf and put them on my desk. I study Mike's handwriting, neat and crisp as it always was. I reread his catalogued notes—the dates and facts and questions that I've come to know so well.

No one expected Mike to die young. He was the good brother, after all.

I was the troubled one in my family: the stereotypical middle child who never fit in, whose moods swung wildly. The fourth son in a family of seven sons, I was constantly looking for attention and love. I was the lost brother who'd spent time in mental institutions. I never thought I would live to see my twenty-first birthday.

It took me three decades to rewire my brain in order to reject the lessons of my past and figure out a way to keep on living.

The "Salient Facts" document reads like a reconstructed diary. Mike had carefully listed dates and activities and symptoms that he was experiencing in order to help his doctor determine the best course of treatment. In the entry for December 15, 1991–January 15, 1992, Mike writes, "very tired, common cold like symptoms that wouldn't leave—didn't miss work & continued to swim one mile 3x/week—made an appointment with Dr. S. for complete annual physical." Dr. S. was Mike's internist at NYU Medical.

During the same time period, I was living in Washington, D.C., selling men's shoes at Nordstrom. As Mike's symptoms of HIV/AIDS were first appearing, I was in the midst of another nervous breakdown—part of a string of breakdowns that lasted throughout my late teens and twenties.

At the end of 1991, I'd been dating one of my coworkers. He sold men's accessories at Nordstrom: suspenders, socks, cuff links. We worked across the aisle from one another. He was impeccably dressed. Throughout our shifts, I'd glance over to watch him show a customer how to tie a real bowtie. When I went on my break, I'd ask him if I could bring him back anything—a latte, maybe, or a cinnamon bun. At the end of the day, I'd wait until he'd finished straightening up his area so that we could leave together, taking the Metro back into the city. I hoped that we'd spend the night together or at least grab a drink. He rarely took me up on my offers, saying that he wasn't thirsty or hungry, or that he'd already made after-work plans. When we did hang out, I was so happy that my enthusiasm annoyed him. He called me hyperactive and told me to calm down. (I hated it when people told me to calm down. When they did, I felt like a misbehaving child.) Still, I thought we were building a life together, one that valued hard work, loyalty, and an appreciation for a well-tailored suit.

One day during the after-Christmas Sales Event, he told me that I was too needy. While he stood there straightening ties, he said to me that I was looking for more than a boyfriend. He said that I wanted a savior, and he couldn't take the pressure. He wasn't wrong, even if I couldn't see it at the time.

When he broke up with me, I felt the weight of all the other men whom I dated and who inevitably broke up with me for similar reasons. The flaw wasn't with them, I'd suddenly realized, but with me. I was the problem, and I had no idea how to fix me.

After work, I took the Metro back to my basement apartment. I took a knife from the kitchen drawer and locked myself in my bathroom. I looked in the mirror and saw someone that I hated. I told my reflection that I deserved to die. I held the knife in my right hand. I turned my left hand over and flexed my wrist so that the vein popped to the surface. I ran the tip of the knife along the vein. The knife was dull, however, and I only scraped some skin off my wrists. (Later, the doctor would call it a "superficial wound," but it was one that produced a faint scar, which still exists to this day.) I looked in the mirror again and saw the same reflection, although I hated it less. Yes, I told myself, I was the problem, but perhaps I wasn't unfixable.

If Mike and I had been close, I would've called him for help. I called a suicide hotline instead.

After checking to see if my insurance was adequate, the man I talked to on the suicide hotline made arrangements for me to fly out to a second-rate clinic in Torrance, California, where I spent ten days with recovering alcoholics and drug addicts.

When one of the clinic nurses checked me in, she asked me the name and number of my closest relative. I thought she meant the person in my family that I felt closest to, and so I gave them Mike's contact information.

Because of the way I was raised, I had a hard time understanding what love was. In our childhood home, love was assumed and never expressed. On the other hand, our dislikes were aired nightly at the dinner table. We disliked fat people because they were lazy. We disliked non-Catholics because they were doomed and too dumb to know it. My father disliked hippies because they thwarted authority. My mother disliked pets because they were filthy. My sister Marie disliked foods that she considered exotic—tomatoes and eggplants and cucumbers. My brothers disliked outsiders. And, with the exception of Mike (I assume), my entire family disliked queer people. Homosexuals, my father used to say in the late 1970s, embodied all that was wrong with the country—the collapse of the nuclear family, the immorality of the sexual revolution, political corruption, perversity, even the quality of TV shows that once were wholesome and clean (*My Three Sons*, *Father Knows Best*, *Leave It to Beaver*) but when we were growing up offered up smut almost every night of the week (*All in the Family*, *Soap*, *Three's Company*).

I grew up knowing that I was queer and that if my family ever found out, they'd despise me. I could never reconcile the assumption that my family loved me with the knowledge that they also hated queer people like me.

At the end of 1991 while I was in the clinic in California, Mike called me. His phone call was the clearest expression of love I'd ever felt from anyone in my family. I was excited about his call. I felt like a bullied child and Mike had come to rescue me.

I was giddy on the phone. Mike was matter-of-fact. Clinical, almost. Perhaps he thought I was in a delicate state and he was being careful not to excite me.

I stood in a hallway across from the nurses' station where a phone for patients hung on the wall. In the clinic, privacy was discouraged, and so everyone could hear everyone else's phone calls. Some people cupped their hands over the receiver and kept their voices low in an attempt at intimacy. I didn't, however. When Mike called, I wanted everyone in the clinic to know that I was talking to my brother and that my brother loved me, so I talked loud enough to be overheard.

The louder I talked, however, the softer Mike spoke so that a couple of times I had to ask him to repeat what he said.

"Mom said what?" I asked.

"She misses you," he said in a whisper.

"Oh," I said. "Tell her I'm all right."

He muttered something I couldn't understand. "What?" I shouted.

"OK. I'll tell her," he said a little louder.

During our conversation, we didn't talk about my suicide attempt. Neither did I bother to ask Mike how he was doing. Instead, we gossiped about our siblings—the stability of their marriages, the number of children they were having, the ways they were becoming like our parents. He talked about how cold it was back East, and I gloated that the weather in California was gorgeous.

"I might move here," I told him.

"Good for you," he said.

According to the "Salient Facts" document, on February 5, 1992, Mike saw Dr. S., who reassured him that he "was one of his healthiest patients." By the time of his appointment, Mike's fatigue and cold-like symptoms had disappeared.

Every day at the clinic in Torrance, the routine for me was the same. In the morning, we lined up by the nurses' station for our meds and for the nurses to check our vitals. (They told me I was in excellent health.) We ate breakfast together in the dining hall, and then headed off to group therapy—the alcoholics in one therapy session, the drug addicts in another, and the rest of us with depression and anxiety disorders in a third. We stayed in group therapy until lunchtime, telling our stories to the resident psychologist, who was tough. When I became despondent because I refused to believe that my life would ever get better than it was at that moment, the psychologist called me out, saying that my despondency was just a way to get attention. He wasn't wrong. After lunch, we met individually with our assigned therapists. My therapist was a young guy named Gerry—he insisted that I call him Gerry and not Dr. Wells. He wore oversized glasses and triple-pleated pants. He liked to hold our sessions while we walked around the clinic's grounds. Then, in the late afternoon there was some kind of creative arts therapy project—painting or ceramics or knitting. If we were into knitting (I was). In the evening after dinner, we watched brat pack movies: *The Breakfast Club*, *St. Elmo's Fire*, *Pretty in Pink*.

Gerry was a cognitive therapist. I'd never heard of cognitive therapy. The idea behind cognitive therapy, according to Gerry, was to change my behavior by changing my thought patterns. I never thought of my brain as something that could be changed. I thought that it had been preloaded with all the software I'd ever need.

My mother liked to boast that we were a family with mathematical brains, and I accepted her declaration without question. When I was young, however, and wanted to be a writer, I couldn't reconcile this artistic desire with the analytical brain that was the hallmark of our family. I felt that this creative impulse was a sign that something was wrong with me, that there was a virus in my brain's software.

After ten days in the clinic, I returned to D.C. Gerry, however, suggested that I move to California so that he could continue working with me. He said that a completely different environment might act like geographic shock treatment that would help begin to rewire my brain.

As Mike was getting his clean bill of health, I was driving across the country, maxing out my credit cards on gas and cheap motels and fried foods. I took the southern route from D.C. through Nashville, Memphis, Oklahoma City, Albuquerque, and finally into Los Angeles. The farther I got from D.C.—and from the Midwest where I grew up—the more confident I felt that I'd turned a corner, that death and thoughts of dying were evaporating, as if just seeing the Grand Canyon and the bright colors of the Arizona desert, or driving up and over the San Bernardino Mountains and seeing the Pacific Ocean were enough to make everything right.

By the time I arrived in California, Mike was in London and Paris for business. He writes in the document that he'd been "subjected to a lot of stress at work—pressure to complete an intellectually challenging paper on international tax law that was to be published in a journal." When he arrived in London, the fatigue he'd experienced at the end of the year returned, but he blamed it on jet lag. Regardless of how he was feeling, he bought poppers (a popular nitrate in the gay club scene) and went out to a club where he picked up a guy and had sex. The poppers seemed to worsen his condition, he writes, and so he threw them away.

By the time he got to Paris, Mike was so sick he could barely speak. His throat was swollen. A doctor prescribed a dose of penicillin, which cleared up his sore throat and restored his voice, but did nothing for his fatigue.

Back in New York, Mike's cold turned into the flu. He went to the emergency room at St. Vincent's, where they did a complete checkup, including chest X-rays. They found that he was severely dehydrated, and gave him fluids intravenously. The doctor's analysis stated that, as Mike records, "'but for the fact that I was a gay man' they would have thought that all I had was a case of the flu." They recommended that Mike get tested for HIV and Pneumocystis pneumonia (PCP), but he ignored this recommendation. Dr. S. had already tested him for HIV, although the results hadn't come back yet.

In California, I found a job as a secretary at the University of California in Irvine. I rented an apartment in Laguna Beach, twelve miles south of the campus. The apartment was on a cliff just up from the Pacific Coast Highway. It wasn't really an apartment, but rather a makeshift room created by the owner of the house by cordoning off the back part of the garage. I rented the makeshift apartment because it was cheap, and because it had a large deck with a 180-degree view of the Pacific Ocean. When I wasn't working—or seeing Gerry—I sat on that deck, looking out across the water, or I was down at the beach teaching myself to body surf.

I'd never lived in a landscape like California. My childhood was spent in the flatlands of the Midwest, where the monotony of cornfields and suburbs mirrored a Midwestern ideology that shunned difference and discouraged exploration of any kind: personal or geographic. In Laguna Beach, the landscape swept down from the Niguel Hills and rolled onto the beach and stretched out in the arc of the ocean's horizon. I thought that if I stayed long enough in California—if I spent enough time on that deck and down at the beach—I could erase my past and replace it with a future based on movement and exploration and discovery. In California, I thought that I could heal.

Back in New York, on the other hand, Mike was getting sicker. The entry in the document for March 20, 1992–April 10, 1992 reads: "fatigue, sleeplessness, muscle ache, sore dry parched throat, persistent dry cough, weakness, rapid onset of the symptoms in a more severe fashion on an 8 day cycle & severe form would last a day or two—did not miss work, continued to swim." Dr. S. prescribed Biaxin, an antibiotic, which cleared up Mike's symptoms for two or three days but then the eight-day cycle returned.

Every morning in California, I woke up as the sun rose and made coffee in the Mr. Coffee that sat on a small wooden table on the deck. I had no kitchen, just a hot plate, which was next to the Mr. Coffee, and a mini-refrigerator, which was shoved under the table. I ate Pop Tarts for breakfast and Tuna Helper for dinner. I made too little money to go out to restaurants or bars. I hadn't come to California to socialize. Instead, I thought of myself as a hermit who avoided people when I could, and spent as much time by myself, sitting in silence and allowing the toxins of my past to leech out of me as if it were an infection that needed sunlight and sea air to heal.

At work, I spent the day answering phones and filing paperwork and writing memos for my boss. I affected a convivial but aloof persona to keep my coworkers at a distance.

"I'd love to go out for drinks after work, but I have plans," I'd say when one of my coworkers asked me to join them for happy hour. "Maybe next time."

Twice a week after work, I saw Gerry. His office was in a strip mall in Torrance, which was completely out of the way. But I thought he could help me figure out the reasons I'd spent so much of my life wanting to die, and to find ways to never let that happen again. We talked about how different I felt from my brothers; how lonely my childhood had been; how I'd had a hard time fitting in. Gerry taught me about "rooftop chatter"—the continuous dialogue of negative thoughts that played in my head. He taught me to recognize the patterns that sent me down the dark holes I couldn't help but fall into. He helped me to look for triggers in my life that set my mind into a tailspin: criticism of any kind, no matter how seemingly inconsequential ("You're so Midwestern"); fat jokes, even if they weren't directed at me; and, the guttural sound of my father's voice, even when it came out of men I didn't know.

On those days I wasn't seeing Gerry, I left work and drove back to my apartment, where I'd quickly change into a swimsuit and flip-flops and race down to the beach, grabbing every bit of sun that I could before it set. I quickly lost my Midwestern paleness and became tan and healthy looking. My brown hair turned blond. On the beach, I sat by myself near an outcrop of boulders that I felt protected me from others. I stayed on the beach for hours listening to the Cowboy Junkies and George Michael and Rick Astley on my Walkman.

Later, I'd eat Tuna Helper while I sat on the deck in an Adirondack chair that faced out over the tree canopy and out farther to the ocean. I waited until the sun set and the last remnants of light left the sky, until my landlord put his two small children to bed and turned off the lights, until the stars came out and all that was left was the darkness and the sound of the sea coming in and going out.

For the first time in my life, I felt the comfort of solitude, which was different than the loneliness I'd felt growing up. My loneliness was filled with anxiety and fear, while the solitude I found in Laguna was calm and peaceful. I began to be comfortable being alone with myself, when in the past I feared silence, thinking that in the empty space that was created when words and thoughts ceased, memory would creep in and make it impossible for me to live.

In May of 1992, Mike saw a specialist, who diagnosed Mike with chronic fatigue syndrome (CFS), or the "yuppie flu," as it was called in the '90s. Mike's internist thought CFS was a made-up disease and told Mike, according to the document, "what I really needed was to quit my job and move to a Caribbean island for a few years because I was too intense & that he saw many stressed out Wall Street lawyers but I was at the extreme."

A month later, Mike records a new group of symptoms. "Once," he writes, "while swimming, once after sex, my heart felt for about 30 seconds like I was having a heart attack—this scared me a lot." In addition to his heart palpitations, Mike felt "tingling all around my brain or head." He also had flashes of pain in his ankles, knees, hips, and elbows. At one point that June, he writes, he thought he could feel "something move throughout my entire body."

A woman whom I'd known in Washington, D.C., had also moved to California. Her name was Savannah. She'd moved to Balboa Island with her boyfriend, a frat boy who'd gotten a job as a sports promoter. Their house was filled with cutouts of professional football players holding sports drinks, stacks of basketball jerseys, and crates of beer glasses etched with the logos of professional baseball teams.

Savannah easily adapted to California life. While her boyfriend traveled around the country for work, she kept the house in order and created a social network around her so that she was never bored. She was constantly inviting me to brunches and parties and benefits so that she could introduce me to people she found interesting. I hated the idea and instead agreed to one-on-one lunch dates and movie nights on her couch. But that was usually it.

Over the Fourth of July weekend in 1992, however, she convinced me to go with her to a party where everyone would be dressed in white. She rented a vintage car, and we drove around Newport Beach as if we were characters in *The Great Gatsby*. I played along with Savannah and her handsome friends that day. We drank Old Fashioneds and Gimlets and dry martinis. We played croquet and badminton. We ate our dinner from cloth-lined picnic baskets and drank champagne from stemmed glassware as we watched fireworks go off over the bay. The whole time, I felt as if I were playing the part of someone who liked to socialize when I didn't. I only wanted to get back to the solitude of my deck and my private view out over the ocean.

That same Fourth of July weekend, Mike was in Seattle, Washington, for the International Gay & Lesbian Aquatic

Championship. I imagine that he swam the 50-meter freestyle and the individual medley and the 100-meter backstroke, events he used to compete in when we were young. In the document, he writes, "felt horrible & was scared even though I did compete although poorly." He gives a list of symptoms he experienced in Seattle: fatigue, problems with his gait and balance, tingling in his fingers, severe nausea, and heart irregularities. When he returned to New York, he told his psychiatrist Dr. R. what had happened in Seattle. Dr. R. was convinced that Mike had Lyme disease, as he himself had had Lyme disease and experienced similar symptoms.

On August 4, 1992, Mike writes, "I panicked because my chest felt so horrible at work. I left, went home & called Dr. S., he was on vacation & so I saw his partner Dr. K. I feared that I had PCP, he told me I was being ridiculous & that there was no way this was HIV." Dr. K. diagnosed Mike with a spastic esophagus.

Two days later, Mike saw Dr. L., one of the leading experts on Lyme disease, according to the *New York Times*. For an hour and a half, Mike talked with Dr. L. about the physical problems he'd been experiencing. Dr. L. agreed with Mike's psychiatrist that he probably had Lyme disease and took blood to confirm his diagnosis. He prescribed large doses of Minocin—another antibiotic—but warned Mike that he might have strange reactions. "I did," Mike writes. "I had a little rash and mild hallucinations."

I'd stopped seeing Gerry by the middle of the summer. Our sessions had gone beyond talking about my childhood and the lessons I'd learned that had messed up my head. Instead, he began experimenting with an electroencephalogram machine, which he attached to my head in order to map by brainwaves. It felt too Dr. Frankenstein for me. Gerry didn't take my discomfort seriously—he said it was just another thought pattern that I needed to rewrite. Besides, I'd grown bored with therapy and needed a break. I knew that I was better off having seen Gerry. I no longer thought about dying, at least I didn't think about it constantly. I thought that I'd made it through the darkest period of my life, and that I was going to be okay.

By August of 1992, I was beginning to feel restless in my self-imposed hermitage. Despite Savannah's ongoing efforts to introduce me to friends and set me up on dates—which I never went on—I kept to myself. I had become used to solitude, but solitude was also beginning to feel like stasis, and stasis was the motto my family lived by: stay close to home, stay put, stay on the straight and narrow. After being in California for eight months, I felt the need to move.

On a Friday night in late August—after Savannah had invited me to a bonfire party on the beach, and I had turned her down—I sat on the deck of my apartment looking out over the Pacific. I heard my landlord and his two young children laughing and playing a game.

I was restless. I felt that if I sat in that chair a moment longer my body was going to revolt and force me to bolt off the deck, run down to the beach, and swim out into the ocean as far as I could go before growing too tired to make it safely back to shore.

I could have gone to Savannah's party—telling her that I'd changed my mind—or I could've gone to the one gay bar within driving distance. But I didn't like the place the one time I visited—too many California pretty boys in their polo shirts and ironed shorts and boat shoes, and too much boasting about their cars and houses and the waves they'd surfed. I could have pulled out my notebook and worked on one of the screenplays I'd been trying to write, thinking that I could make it as a screenwriter in Los Angeles. Instead, I decided to give myself a haircut.

I had hair then—I'm almost bald now—and I used to go to Supercuts up the highway. I asked myself, how hard could it be to cut my own hair? Wet it down, draw up a few strands between my fingers, and snip off the ends. Simple.

I went into my small, dimly lit bathroom. I took off my shirt and I stuck my head under the shower to get my hair wet. I stood in front of the bathroom mirror with a pair of scissors and a comb. "You can do this," I said out loud. I started at the crown of my head, made a part with the comb, drew up a row of hair and cut off the top two inches. I was pleased with myself when I saw the snippets of hair fall into the sink. The cutting went smoothly for a while, but then it all went to hell. The hair on the right side of my head looked longer than the left, and every time I tried to even them out, the asymmetry got worse.

I tried to cut the hair at the back of my head by touch—starting at the nape and working my way up. I tried to see the progress I'd made by standing with my back to the mirror and turning my head slowly around, hoping to catch a glimpse of the back of my head in the mirror. It was a disaster. There were near-bald patches dotting the back of my head, and long strands that hung down behind my ears. I looked as if I had some disease and my hair was falling out from the treatment.

I stared at my reflection in the mirror. The hate and self-pity that had caused me to take that dull knife across my wrists came flooding back to me. It felt as if all those hours sitting on that deck and watching the calm waters of the ocean, staying quiet and imagining a new kind of life, cocooning myself away until something new and better and beautiful emerged, had all been wasted. I was an idiot, I told myself. I was a fool. I couldn't escape my past any more than most people could.

At the same time that I was verging on another nervous breakdown in Laguna Beach, Mike was going to visit another doctor—his fifth in eight months.

In one of the tests that had been performed on Mike, a doctor noted elevated levels of anticardiolipin antibodies and recommended Mike see a specialist, Dr. B., who practiced out of Cornell Medical Center. When she saw Mike—as he reports in his document—"she said she did not believe I had Lyme but probably HIV since this phenomenon is seen in the AIDS population—she recommended I retest for HIV. Dr. L. had retested me but claims the state lost my results."

In the margins of the document, Mike quotes a Johns Hopkins book, which he doesn't name: "Less than 1% of the people who take the HIV test receive a false positive result. This can be due to medical conditions which have nothing to do with HIV/AIDS." Dr. R., Mike's psychiatrist, told Mike of one of his patients who'd tested positive for HIV although she had Lyme instead. Her story was told in a *Redbook* article dated March 1992.

Instead of just stabbing myself in the neck with the scissors that I'd used to cut my own hair—or worse, returning to my family in Indianapolis—I called an old friend, John, who was living in South Bend, Indiana, after having graduated from the MFA program in writing at Notre Dame. I'd known John from Indianapolis where we'd met at a gay bar. We both wanted to be writers—and both had histories of nervous breakdowns.

I told John that I was feeling desperate, and he ordered me to drive to South Bend immediately so that he could watch over me. Feeling as if I had little choice, I threw some clothes in a bag. I called my boss and left a voice message saying that I had to return home because of a family emergency. I hopped into my truck and headed back East.

I drove north up through Las Vegas and Salt Lake City, and then turned east through Omaha and Des Moines and Iowa City and Chicago, and straight into South Bend. Unlike my drive west eight months earlier, driving back to Indiana felt like a defeat. I'd worked so hard to get Indiana out of my head, and now I was heading back there. Driving from California to Indiana felt like a death march. I was exhausted by the time I arrived in South Bend.

John worked the front desk of a motel, which sat on the banks of the St. Joseph River. The motel was part of a "gay resort" that a local man had bought and hoped to brand as a place where the gay community could feel safe. Along with the motel, there was a bar named Truman's that was located in one of the adjacent old factory buildings.

It was early in the evening when I drove into the gravel parking lot of the gay resort in South Bend. John had a few more hours on his shift at the front desk. He told me to wait for him up at the bar.

"The bartender's name is David," John told me. "He'll take care of you."

The bar had brick walls and tall ceilings. Through an arched masonry opening, I saw a room with a pool table and a dance floor. I walked in and sat at the bar, which was nearly empty. The bartender, David, was sexy. He was thin and had wavy dark hair. He wore a black silk vest, black Army boots, and bike chains around his neck. He wore a dozen bracelets on each wrist. I liked him immediately.

"John sent me," I said, trying to sound mysterious.

"He did, did he?" David said, putting his right leg up on the bar well and leaning toward me.

"Yeah," I said.

David grabbed a bottle of beer and placed it in front of me.

"Nice haircut," he said.

At first, I thought that David was making fun of me in the same way my brothers would have. But there was nothing dismissive or dangerous in the sound of David's voice.

"I did it myself," I said, running my hands through my hair.

"I can tell," he said. "It's cool."

When I was a junior in high school, I went to the local mall and got a perm. My hair had always been straight and thin, and the woman who sat me in her chair convinced me that a perm would give my hair some body. I was adventurous enough then to say "yes." When I got home and my father saw what I'd done, he said, "I never thought a son of mine would do a thing like that." My brothers laughed at me, calling me a girl. My mother shook her head in disapproval. My sister Marie stifled a giggle. I immediately went out to the drugstore and bought a relaxer to take the perm out. My father looked askance at me for a long time, trying to figure out what kind of son I was. He was not the only one. My brothers kept their eyes on me, trying to figure out if I was normal. My judgmental family was always slapping me back in line.

The moment I met David, I felt a shift in me. Perhaps it was because he paid attention to me. Or perhaps because at my lowest—with that horrible haircut and those missteps in my life that had me thinking it was better to die than continually face disappointment—David took one look at me and just accepted what he saw. No one had ever done that before.

It took me three days to seduce David away from his boyfriend—a conquest I've never let David forget, and one he dismisses. "It wasn't really a relationship, you know," David likes to say now, but I don't believe him. David's ex-boyfriend was an alcoholic, David explains when I tell this story to friends. The ex would pass out on the couch long before the evening was over, and long before there was any chance of having sex.

Because I was happy to have met David, and because I felt that something had changed in my life, I called Mike in New York.

When we spoke, Mike didn't tell me about the medical issues he'd been dealing with over the past eight months. He didn't tell me about the constant fatigue or the flu he couldn't shake. He didn't recount his time in London and Paris when he had the worst case of strep throat he'd ever experienced. He didn't tell me about the creatures he felt crawling up his spine, or the heart murmurs or the brain fever. He said nothing about the eight doctors he'd seen in the past year, or about the diagnoses he'd gotten from them: chronic fatigue syndrome and Lyme disease and work-related stress. He didn't tell me about the constant anxiety he felt.

Perhaps Mike heard the excitement in my voice and didn't want to ruin whatever fun I was having. Perhaps he was too frightened by the idea that he might be HIV positive to confide in me.

"Well, life is great for me, too," Mike said instead. "Couldn't be happier."

After spending two weeks with John (and David) in South Bend, I got into my truck and headed back to California. There was a lot to think about. I knew that if I really wanted to change my life and live differently than the way my family had taught me, I couldn't make the change on my own. I needed someone's help, someone like David.

By the time I pulled into Cheyenne, I knew that I could go back to the kind of life I was living—one in which I felt I was always trying to keep my head above water—or I could take a chance with David. The choice was crystal clear to me. It was one of those rare moments in life when the future seems easily discernable.

I stopped in a drugstore in Cheyenne and bought a postcard—David had told me it was his birthday when I left South Bend. The card had a pale blue background with crude hand-drawings of arrowheads and frontier women and Native Americans and cattle and cowboys and mountains and streams. In the center of the post-card was the outline of the state of Montana. On the reverse, I wrote in green pen, "I know this postcard says Montana but I'm really in Wyoming . . . it's all the same. I just liked the postcard. The drive has been extremely boring until I got to the Rockies, now it's pretty cool. I hope you had a great birthday today. Thinking of you, Andy."

I dropped the postcard in the mail. After all those years of wondering what it meant to love, I thought I'd finally figured it out. I simply had to choose to love. I had to take a chance. This time, I told myself, I was going to love this person even if I barely knew him.

A few weeks after I returned to my small apartment and my lonely deck, I got a handmade postcard in the mail from David. It was a pencil drawing of a heart sitting on a field of green with a blue sky above it. On the reverse side, David had written, "The sky was blue / Like this today / And the grass so green / My heart, like the wind clear and light / Floats from earth to sky." Almost every day for a month, I received a handmade postcard in the mail from David.

We began talking regularly on the phone. We talked about starting a life together. David flew out to Laguna Beach for a long weekend. We drove up to Los Angeles to visit his sister and her family. We talked about our pasts, about being gay in America at a time when it wasn't easy for gay people to live openly. We talked about our families. I told him about the breakdowns I'd had. He told me how difficult it was to come out to his family. I told him about Mike.

I thought David would be good for me and that I'd be good for him. While I was impulsive and overemotional, David was more grounded and steady. While I was loud at times, he was mostly soft-spoken. While I tended to be antisocial, he made friends easily. And where he tended to get stuck and had a hard time figuring out how to move on, I was eager for change and willing to take risks. Where he held back, I pushed forward.

On September 16, 1992, Mike sought the recommendation from the Gay Men's Health Crisis (GMHC) on where to get a reliable HIV test—he didn't trust his internist to retest him. GMHC recommended Personal Diagnostics because he would get his test results in forty-eight hours. Personal Diagnostics performed the Elisa & Western blot test on Mike, one of the most reliable HIV tests at the time. Two days later, he got his results. Mike writes, "my boyfriend with whom I'd been monogamous for 6 months & with whom I'd done sexually the same things I'd always done that might put him or me at risk . . . we were both tested for HIV—he tested negative and I tested positive."

A week later, Mike saw Dr. S., his internist, who was shocked to learn of Mike's HIV status. According to the "Salient Facts" document, Dr. S. said to Mike, "he would have bet his house that I wouldn't become positive." Dr. S. also told Mike that the HIV test was almost 100% accurate and that "I shouldn't hold out hope that another foreign substance was causing the positive results."

During one of the phone conversations David and I had, I suggested that I move to South Bend and we live together. David didn't hesitate to say yes. I gave notice at work and to my landlord. I packed up my belongings—I didn't have much. I sat on my deck for one last time, looked out over the ocean, and knew that it was time for me to leave it behind. I'd miss it, I thought, but I couldn't stay sitting there forever.

I sold my truck to one of Savannah's friends. Savannah drove me to the airport. She thought that I was crazy for picking up my life and moving in with someone I barely knew. She wouldn't hug me at the gate, but instead crossed her arms and said that I'd be back sooner than I thought. I knew that I wouldn't. I was certain that this part of my life was over—as was my friendship with Savannah—and that a new one was beginning.

On November 9, 1992, in the middle of a snowstorm, I landed in Chicago, where David met me. We drove to his apartment in South Bend—each of us a little nervous—and began our life together. Almost from the beginning, Mike's absence has been an integral part of my relationship with David.

At the end of the "Salient Facts" document, Mike lists a series of questions he posed to his doctors. He asks, "For my own peace of mind, how do you think I caught HIV infection?" Mike details his sexual history and, except for a few risky sexual encounters in college, he insists that he'd only ever practiced safe sex. He wonders if he doesn't have both HIV and Lyme, and asks how to treat both diseases. He wonders if he should avoid riding the subway for fear of contracting tuberculosis. In question number 4—which he highlighted with two asterisks—he writes, "I have so much fear of AIDS dementia or Lyme dementia, is there anything preventative to do now especially since something has been going on in my brain/CNS for about 6 months now?"

There are, of course, no answers given in this document. There are only facts and questions and suppositions.

Mike and David met a few times before Mike died. They got along well enough; although, David easily saw through Mike's bullshit, and Mike knew it. Mike didn't tease David the way Mike liked to tease me. Mike didn't try to prove that he was smarter than David, even though he might have been, the way Mike was always trying to show me that I was his intellectual subordinate. Mike didn't get under David's skin the way Mike could so easily get under mine. When I saw the two of them together, I knew that David was exactly the right person for me, a protector against my own brother's arrogance.

Mike never told me that he was sick. He never told me that he was in trouble or that he needed help. The last time I saw him, he acted as if everything was normal, as if his life was as happy as mine.

In the loft of our house in upstate New York, I flip through the pages of the "Salient Facts" document one more time. I look at Mike's familiar handwriting. I see the dates lined up along the left-hand margin. I reread those unanswered questions at the end of the document. I line the sheets up neatly, smoothing out their edges.

Downstairs, I hear David mixing martinis. It's 6:00 and we never miss cocktail hour.

"Are you done yet?" he calls up to me.

"Be there in a minute," I say.

I put the document back in the shelf between two books: *The Carnivorous Lamb* by Agustín Gómez-Arcos and *A Boy's Own Story* by Edmund White. I turn off the desk lamp and go downstairs.

Familial Bodies

When I met my parents at the medical examiner's office on Thirtieth Street and First Avenue in Manhattan in the fall of 1993, a receptionist escorted us into a small waiting room. My father paced back and forth in the room, his soft-soled shoes squeaking on the linoleum. My mother and I sat across from each other in blue plastic chairs. The room was cold.

My father is a big man with a beer gut and thick arms. He was a football player in high school and college. I have a photo of him taken after a game. He looks like a lineman who could easily break through the line of scrimmage.

With each lap across the room it seemed that my father's body grew larger, expanding into the empty spaces between the three of us.

My mother is thin as she always has been and probably always will be. She is strong and independent, though, and has taught her children to be aggressive and demanding. In that room, she seemed to shrink in direct proportion to my father's expansion. Their grief pushed and pulled between them like a lunar tide.

I sat there anticipating the moment when we'd be taken to see Mike's corpse. What I knew of that moment came from TV crime dramas: the body covered in a white sheet, the grieving relatives standing next to it, the attendant pulling back the sheet, the moment of revelation, the gasps.

I was resentful that my parents were with me. I wanted to believe that Mike belonged only to me: two gay brothers comforting each other from having grown up in a conservative family. I wanted his death to belong to me and only me. I didn't think then that I was being mean or selfish. I only knew how hard it was for Mike (and me) to escape Indianapolis. And I knew that my parents would take Mike's body back there for burial. I didn't think that he'd want that, but there was little I could do to stop them.

My father's pacing came from his inability to process emotions, as if his emotions were a dish he couldn't digest. He'd always been this way. When we were kids my six brothers, my sister Marie, and I would be arguing around the dinner table about silly things—who broke the chain on one of our bicycles, who cheated at a game of Monopoly—and my father would sit there quietly listening to us until his patience wore out. Then, his face would tighten and his body would tense up until he couldn't hold it in any longer. He'd suddenly scream at us to be quiet or bang his fist on the table. He did this all the time, but each time we were shocked by his anger.

At the morgue, my father's pacing annoyed me. I wanted to tell him to stop and sit down, but I've never been bold enough to tell him to do anything. At one point, my father did stop. He came over and stood in front of me. I looked up at him. I could feel heat coming off of his body.

"Anyone who lives this way deserves to die this way," he said, looking directly at me.

I felt ashamed, as if I'd been the cause of Mike's death. I turned away from my father. I would like to say that my father's condemnation surprised me. I would like to say that it made me angry. But I wasn't surprised, and I wasn't angry. It was exactly the kind of thing my father would say. At least the father I'd always known.

Over the years, my brothers and sister have argued with me that my father was too consumed with grief and didn't know what he was saying at the morgue. They question whether he said it at all. They think I have an overly active imagination that exaggerates the truth. Besides, they assure me that my father loves me as if these secondhand declarations of love are enough to erase the memory of my father telling me that I deserved to end up like Mike.

My mother whispered sharply to my father, "Oh, hush, Frank."

My father returned to his pacing.

I watched him walk to the other side of the room, hoping that he'd walk out the door and leave the identification process to my mother and me. He didn't.

Soon, a tall woman with dark skin walked into the room. She wore a blue lab coat and carried a clipboard. My father stopped moving. My mother stood up and steeled herself for this moment. I stood up too and moved toward the door, expecting to be taken to where Mike's body was being kept. The woman, however, invited us to sit down. Her voice was calm and soothing. She gave us her condolences, which my mother accepted with a hesitant nod. My father said nothing.

The woman took a Polaroid from her clipboard. The metal clip snapped back in place when she pulled it out. She handed the photo to my mother. I leaned over and looked over her shoulder.

The Polaroid was a close up of Mike's face, which was swollen and discolored from lividity. It looked like he'd had an allergic reaction to a bee sting or a spider bite. The swelling was a sickly yellow-green that covered the left side of his face, spreading up and over his nose and lips and eyes. He was barely recognizable. My mother and I, however, saw the way his hairline arched at its widow's peak and fell into the soft curve at the center point of his forehead, and knew that it was Mike.

When my mother handed the Polaroid to my father, who had refused to sit down, he didn't recognize him.

"I can't tell," he said. "I can't tell."

My father held the picture tightly as if he could squeeze Mike's image out of it.

"Aren't we going to see his body?" I asked the medical examiner.

She said that the photo was enough, but I was disappointed. I wanted to see his body, to touch his cold skin. I thought it might make what felt unreal more believable.

My mother took the photo from my father and handed it back to the woman, who fastened it beneath the clip.

"It's him," my mother said.

My father crossed his arms over his chest and refused to agree with my mother.

When Mike's body was sent back to Indianapolis for burial, I went to the funeral home to ask the director if I could see the corpse.

The funeral home was familiar to me. I'd passed it every day when I was a kid on my way to school. It looked ordinary then: a red brick building with columns at the entrance and tall windows that looked no different from the office building next to it. When I pulled into the parking lot of the Flanner & Buchanan Shadeland Mortuary, it took on a new significance. Somewhere inside the building, Mike's body laid waiting for us to bury it.

When I walked in the front door, the funeral home was empty. No services were being held. The staff, I assumed, was somewhere behind closed doors getting bodies ready for burial. At the entrance, there was a low desk with a vase of flowers and a stack of business cards. The place smelled of cleaning solvents as if the carpets had recently been shampooed.

I waited by the desk for the funeral director. When he came out from the back, I introduced myself and asked to see Mike's body. He shook his head and said that I couldn't see him. He said that the body was in bad condition, but he didn't elaborate.

I didn't care what Mike's body looked like—I imagined decaying flesh and sunken eye sockets and the sutures on his torso where he'd been opened and emptied and catalogued and put back together. But I didn't know how to explain to the director that I felt a need to see Mike's body. I needed to see what death looked like, how it had hollowed out the essence of Mike and left behind the remnants. I needed to understand what it meant to die, if for no other reason than to prove to myself that living was better. But I didn't get the chance to see Mike's body, and so grief found a comfortable place inside of me where it's been ever since.

Twenty-three years after Mike's death in 2016, I returned to the medical examiner's office in Manhattan. Along with the suggestion that I retrieve the police report concerning Mike's death, my shrink had suggested that reading Mike's autopsy report might help me deal with my grief.

It felt strange walking into that building again, the memory of the waiting room came back to me instantly.

As did my father's condemnation: "Anyone who lives this way deserves to die this way."

Requesting the autopsy report was simple. I filled out some paperwork and waited for the report to arrive in the mail. During the few weeks I had to wait, I imagined what the report would contain. I thought that maybe there'd be a copy of the Polaroid used to identify him. I wondered if there'd be photos of the autopsy itself: Mike's sternum cracked open and his ribcage pulled apart and his body splayed as if it were part of an anatomy class. I began to worry there'd be gruesome details about the way he died, the poison eating away at the lining of his stomach and burning holes in his esophagus.

When the report arrived, I opened it and sat down in a chair in my bedroom, resting my elbow on a side table in order to lean over and read it under the light from a small lamp. David was in the front room at his desk working. Our two dogs—Akitas— jumped on the bed and were gnawing on old meat bones.

The autopsy on Mike began at 9:30 A.M. on October 29, 1993, by Dr. Mark Flomenbaum, a different medical examiner from the one who'd showed us the Polaroid.

Dr. Flomenbaum began by examining the external components of Mike's body, noting that it was well developed, well nourished and of average frame: 5'10" and 140 lbs. Mike hadn't weighed that little since before high school. Perhaps, I thought, he'd lost weight in the months before he died.

Dr. Flomenbaum wrote that the color of Mike's hair was brown, which might have been the case in the sterile environment of the morgue where the only light available was from the florescent tubes overhead. But in natural light, it was easy for me to see that Mike's hair had the red hues that came from my mother's Irish ancestry.

The doctor noted that Mike was without a mustache or a beard. He misidentified my brother's eyes as being gray, rather than the green eyes that became translucent at times and opaque at others.

The M.E. noted that Mike had natural teeth in good repair.

The autopsy described Mike's torso as being hirsute and his genitalia as that of a normal circumcised adult male. To a stranger looking at a body, these observations are nothing more than objective facts. For me, however, the description of Mike's body reminds me of mine, of the way our bodies became the locus of so much misunderstanding in a family that condemned homosexuality. It was easy to absorb that hate and to internalize that homophobia. To look in the mirror and see that hirsute torso and those perfectly normal genitalia, and feel disgusted. Even today, I avoid looking at my body in the bedroom mirror, afraid that despite the years between his death and now, I can't escape the past.

Dr. Flomenbaum noted that rigor mortis was mild in Mike's body but that fixed livor was present at the back, upper arms, face, and neck. It was this lividity that had swollen the face we saw in the Polaroid.

The autopsy also said that, "early marbling of the skin is on the shoulders and upper extremities." I imagine Mike's body turning to stone as if he'd seen Medusa. I imagine Mike as a statue that I set in the garden in my house in upstate New York, where I'd see him whenever I went out to harvest the beans or the peas or the small golden tomatoes that come in quickly and drop to the ground before I have a chance to collect them all.

When Dr. Flomenbaum finished his external examination, he began to examine the inside of Mike's body. He started with the head, which, he declared, had no contusions or fractures or epidural, subdural, or subarachnoid hemorrhages. He measured Mike's brain at 1580 grams (a little over three pounds), and noted that it was symmetrical with a normal distribution of cranial nerves. He wrote, "the gray and white matter is normally distributed; the ventricular architecture is unremarkable."

The idea that Mike's brain was normal or unremarkable in any way would have offended Mike. If his sexuality caused him pain, the way Mike's brain functioned saved him—at least for a little while. He was the smartest one in our family. When he came home for a visit, he'd cite stories in the *New York Times* when he wanted to prove a point. He'd know what "ventricular architecture" was, and laugh at me for not being able to figure out its definition.

As with his brain, Dr. Flomenbaum found Mike's tongue to be nothing out of the ordinary. From the tongue, and down into the larynx, trachea and esophagus, there was nothing that concerned Dr. Flomenbaum. When he got into the body cavity, though, the damage that caused Mike's death began to reveal itself. The sac around Mike's heart was filled with 75 ml of a straw-colored fluid. The doctor removed Mike's lungs and weighed them—the right was 800 grams while the left 750 grams—and noted that, "both lungs are markedly congested and contain abundant frothy fluid."

Along with the fluid in his lungs, Dr. Flomenbaum noted that there were 60 ml of bile in Mike's stomach, although he saw no discernible fragments of pills or tablets.

My family doesn't want to know the details of Mike's death. For some unexplained reason, my mother believes that Mike fell and hit his head. My father, a good Catholic, believes that the same angels that destroyed Sodom and Gomorrah also took Mike's life. For my siblings, it was enough to know that Mike died, and that the family received his body and deposited it in the ground back home in Indiana. My family would rather not know how Mike died. I want to know every minute detail, thinking that knowing will bring comfort.

It hasn't yet.

When I finished reading the report, I replaced it in its envelope and put it in my desk drawer. I turned off the bedroom light and went into the kitchen to prepare dinner. The dogs followed me, pressing their bodies against my legs the way they do when they sense that I need comforting. David got up from his desk, came over, and put his hand on my shoulder. He let it rest there as

I removed two slippery chicken breasts from their packaging. Then he went back to his desk and the dogs laid down on the floor in the living room.

In the years immediately after Mike died, I visited Indianapolis a few times a year, stopping by the cemetery to stand above his grave and hope that seeing his name etched in granite would assuage the loss that had anchored itself in me. Perhaps because I never got to see Mike's body, I felt disconnected from him when I was at the cemetery. The headstone was just a headstone. And his name was just a name. They had nothing to do with the brother I'd known and lost. If I was looking for Mike at the cemetery, I didn't feel as if he were there. I stopped going to the cemetery eventually and likewise stopped visiting Indianapolis.

Lately, however, I've been returning home, not because I hope to find comfort there—on the contrary, returning to Indianapolis always produces anxiety and unease—but rather, because my father is dying (he has emphysema) and I feel an obligation to see him before he dies. Just like standing over Mike's grave, seeing my father's failing body doesn't evoke the sympathy I imagine it should. Instead I feel detached, as if, on that day in the mortuary, some vital connection between father and son had been severed and could never be rewired.

Last winter, I had a series of telephone conversations with my mother. Her voice was heavy and lethargic, when—as with the rest of my family—her normal voice is energetic and a little too loud. My father, she said, was having a bad winter, the cold was getting into his lungs, and his body seemed to be unable to generate enough warmth to keep him going. She told me that I should plan a trip home to say goodbye.

When my father was first diagnosed with emphysema, he and my mother refused the diagnosis as if the doctors were offering them a choice. They convinced themselves that my father's phlegmatic coughing was due to allergies or, at worse, a slight touch of asthma. My mother especially rejected the idea that my father was sick, because she is strong and healthy, and believes that illness is the result of a weak mind. However, when my father could no longer lie down in bed at night because the compression on his lungs prevented him from breathing, and when throughout the day he had difficulties completing the simplest of tasks—walking from the bedroom to the kitchen, or stepping out of the shower—without having to sit down to catch his breath, my mother reluctantly accepted the diagnosis from his doctors.

I arrived back in Indianapolis in early June in 2015. As I always did when returning home, I planned to stay for two nights before heading back to New York. By the time I arrived, my father had survived the winter and was doing much better. When she picked me up at the airport, my mother said that he'd found a physical therapist who was teaching my father how to increase his lung capacity through a series of breathing exercises.

My father looked no different than the last time I'd seen him—his clumsy body no different than mine. He greeted me at the door with enthusiasm, hugging me in the tentative way we've settled on over the years.

After putting my bag in the bedroom upstairs where I used to sleep as a boy, I walked into the dining room. My father was sitting at the head of the table where he always sat. I never liked talking to my father, but ever since he became ill, I've convinced myself that I should make an effort.

My mother was in the kitchen fixing dinner. She'd invited my siblings and their families over to welcome home the "prodigal son." They use this phrase every time I visit. I cringe when I hear it, as if coming home is a sign of failure that necessitates a feast.

"How's work?" my father asked, as he always asks.

He was wearing a yellow polo shirt, beneath which I saw his once-muscular chest drooping like an old woman's. On his arms were large purple blotches from the bruises he easily gets when any part of his exposed flesh brushes up against any surface. His skin was thin and translucent like velum.

"Fine," I answered, sitting down opposite him in the seat my mother normally occupied. "How are you feeling?"

"Fine," he answered. He was doing the crossword in the local paper—the *Indianapolis Star*—and didn't look up when he spoke, his head down over the paper, his pencil scratching out answers. I stared at his hands. They were so familiar to me from when I was a boy and I used to watch him at his workbench in the garage planing the bottom of a door that stuck in the jam or replacing the worn-out handles on a kitchen cabinet. He has the thick hands of a football player. I looked at my own hands, and as with the rest of my body, they too resembled his, although I was never a football player. I tried to remember what Mike's hands looked like but I've lost the details of his body over the decades and have only retained vague ideas of his appearance: a broad nose and thin lips and a medium build. I thought that, if it were possible to line us up, we'd represent the different stages of the same man aging over time: Mike the fittest one at the time he died; myself the middle-aged man who hasn't yet figured out how to accept his body; and, my father whose body is in the last stages of decline.

Watching him do the crossword, I saw how thin my father's wrists were, which I'd never noticed before. It looked as if beneath the heavy body that I'd always known him to have was a thinner man that I'd never known. My own wrists seemed normal in comparison, except for a very faint scar on my left wrist.

"Your mother tells me that you're looking for a new job," my father said.

"Maybe," I said, pulling out my phone to check emails, and then opening up the *Times* crossword app to look at the clues I hadn't figured out for the day's puzzle.

"Don't you like where you are?" he asked.

"It's not that," I said. "I just want to see what's out there."

I looked up at him. The top of his head was scabby as if he were getting over an infection or had bumped his head on a low-hanging eave or doorway jamb, which he used to do when we were kids.

In addition to inheriting my father's body, I've developed an anxiety disorder that, looking back, resembles the nervous pacing my father displayed at the morgue in Manhattan. During times of stress, my hands shake and my heart races and the muscles in my legs twitch, unable to bear the idea of sitting still.

Stuck in the dining room alone with my father, my body began to quiver. I wanted to think of myself as more mature and less affected by this presence—less haunted by those words he hissed in the morgue back in New York—so I tried to ignore these signs. My body, however, didn't care that I'd been trying to change, and amplified my anxiety until I felt like jumping up from the table and running around the house like a madman.

I couldn't tell if my father knew that I was anxious, and if he took pleasure in knowing this. Maybe he'd take my agitated state as a sign that I wasn't as happy as I pretended to be. Or if he shared my unease and somewhere in his body nervous ticks were playing themselves out despite his best efforts. I've often wondered if he remembered the words he spoke in the morgue, or if his memory was failing along with his body.

Eventually, my mother came in to set the table for dinner. She put her hand on my shoulder as she collected the everyday place-mats in order to set out cloth ones. She understood the tension between my father and me (in the same way she understood the tension that existed between my father and Mike). Over the years, she's tried to broker a truce between us but her efforts haven't been successful.

"Let me help you," I said to my mother, getting up from the table and taking the placemats from her hands.

"I'm fine," my mother said, trying to take the placemats back from me.

"Let him help," my father said.

My mother gave up and walked into the kitchen. I followed her.

My siblings and their families filtered into the house a few hours later. We chitchatted about unimportant things—the weather, local sports teams, work. They asked me how I was doing and I said that I was fine, that life was moving along as it tends to do. They agreed. My nieces and nephews hugged me and welcomed me home. I teased them about how old they were getting. They teased me back. We ate rapidly as we always did—spiral ham on the bone and green bean casserole and dinner rolls and salad with sweet dressing. After eating, we retired into the living room. My brothers watched football on the big-screen TV and I flipped through an old copy of *Newsweek*.

When the game was over, they trickled out of the house and left my parents and me alone. I was sitting on the plaid sofa while my mother was in the La-Z-Boy next to me. My father sat in an overstuffed chair in the corner behind us. He was reading one of the exegetical tracts he subscribed to and read once a day.

"I'm off to bed," he eventually said, struggling to get up out of the chair and shuffling across the living room. "I'll see you in the morning, young man," he said to me before heading down the hall and back toward my parents' bedroom.

"He means well," my mother said when he was gone. She was sipping tea from an old mug.

"I know," I said.

I wanted to believe that my father held no animus toward me, and perhaps he didn't. Perhaps the words he said in the morgue were simply words of grief and not condemnation. Perhaps, I told myself, it was time to forgive him.

I got up from the sofa, wished my mother goodnight, and went upstairs to my old bedroom. I had a tough time sleeping, though. There were too many memories in that bedroom to leave me in peace: the nights I prayed endlessly to be a normal boy, the night I swallowed a half dozen sleeping pills when I knew that my sexual difference was something I couldn't set aside, the nights I wished my father dead so I didn't have to be afraid of him.

In the morning when I walked out of the bedroom door, I heard my father's voice calling me from the room next to mine. I went into the room, which my father had converted into an office—my father is an accountant who's had his own practice for decades and, refusing to retire, still has a few clients. In the middle of the room was a large desk with a credenza. In front of the desk were two chairs for clients to sit in when they came to meet him. I sat in one of the client chairs while he sat behind his desk.

In front of him a ledger book was open. To the right were a calculator and a blue mechanical pencil that he preferred because the lead had a sharp edge and produced the kind of crisp numbers he liked. There were other ledger books stacked on the credenza next to his computer.

"Do you know what this is?" he asked, pointing to the open ledger book. I shook my head. "A client of mine who owns a number of Subway franchises. You can't imagine how much money he makes."

For a half an hour, I sat in my father's office while he chatted about his clients and their financial successes. I was tired and cranky from not having slept, and I couldn't figure out what he was talking about. He couldn't have believed that I cared at all for his clients or his accounting practice. He couldn't have been that obtuse. But then I realized that he knew that I was quick to make excuses to get away from him, and his small talk was a way to keep me a little while longer. I also realized that our conversation, for my father, was a kind of affection. And, I understood, that this was the most affection I'd ever get from him.

If I were a good son, I'd take whatever affection my father was willing to give and excuse the rest. But I am also a brother, who has a duty to protect the memory of a sibling who was lowered into the ground with the curse of his father on his head. I cannot reconcile these two demands.

At one point in his chatting, my father paused. He'd run out of breath and needed to engage one of the exercises his physical therapist had taught him. My father closed his eyes and took in a steady breath, held it for a moment, and then let it out. In that pause, I could've made my escape, or I could've broached the subject of Mike's death, but I didn't do either of these things. Instead, I leaned back in the chair and waited until he'd caught his breath. I felt cruel doing nothing. I thought maybe my presence was torture to him, and I didn't mind torturing him. At that moment, I should've been kind to him, but I chose not to be kind. I should've forgiven him but I've chosen not to forgive. I could've loved him but I've chosen not to.

When my father finished his breathing exercises, he opened his eyes and stared at me.

He said, "You're getting fat. You'd better watch yourself."

I patted my belly, let out a full-throated laugh, and said, "Look who's talking!"

"I'm just telling you the truth," he said as if we'd ever spoken the truth to each other.

"There you have it," I said.

I stood up, turned away from him, and went downstairs to the kitchen where my mother was cooking breakfast.

Prospero's Books

When I was living in Washington, D.C., and Mike lived in New York in the late 1980s and early 1990s, he came to visit me only once. I knew that he'd been to D.C. many times before then for work—he often lobbied Congress as a tax lawyer for Morgan Stanley. But every other time he'd been to D.C., he just rushed into town and then rushed out when he was finished without calling me.

That weekend, however, he called and said he wanted to see me. I didn't know why. I thought that maybe he missed me and finally had time in his busy schedule for a visit.

Once, when I was in my early twenties and still living in Indianapolis, he came home for a weekend visit. (After he left Indianapolis, he rarely came home.) I hoped that he would want to spend some real time with me. I suggested that the two of us go downtown for a fancy lunch at the Rathskeller—one of the oldest restaurants in town—or maybe catch a matinee at the Indianapolis Repertoire Theater. They were my ideas of what kind of life Mike lived in New York—good restaurants and Broadway shows. But he said he wasn't interested. He just wanted to hang around the house and catch up on his sleep.

"It's no big deal," I said offhandedly.

When Mike said he wanted to see me in D.C., I told him that there wasn't any need to spend money on a hotel. There was enough space in my apartment, even though it was a studio apartment. I thought that it would be nice to stay up late talking, and to wake up early and have coffee at the small foldaway table that I kept pushed up against the wall next to the micro-kitchen.

He said that he preferred to stay in a hotel.

"Besides," he said, "money isn't really an issue."

In preparation for Mike's visit to D.C., I made elaborate plans without consulting him. I would meet Mike at his hotel in the morning, and we'd have the continental breakfast in the hotel's restaurant—I convinced myself that this would be much better than having breakfast in my small apartment. I had an image of Mike and me strolling up the Mall—beginning at the Lincoln Memorial, ambling past the Washington Monument and the Smithsonian, and up to the Capitol—as if we were brothers used to spending time together. As if we were intellectual equals discussing democratic politics and contemporary literature and the AIDS epidemic.

I thought it would be nice if we ate lunch at one of the restaurants congressmen and senators dined, like Charlie Palmers or the Bombay Club.

I thought I'd take him to my local gay bar, JR's, for a drink. I imagined us talking openly about men that we saw at the bar that we'd like to have sex with. I imagined us staying out late and drinking too much, stumbling home early in the morning and making too much noise so that the neighbors would yell out their windows for us to be quiet.

When Mike checked into the Park Hyatt, however, he called and said that he only had enough time to spend a few hours with me that Friday night.

"What do you want to do?" I asked him, trying to keep my voice normal.

"It doesn't matter to me," he said. I heard the sound of ice cubes tapping against glass. I thought that he was having a cocktail in his room, looking out of the window at the White House in the distance. Perhaps, he was just having a glass of ice water, parched from a long day at the office and a crowded flight down to D.C.

I suggested we go to a movie and then out to dinner, which, he said, was fine with him.

"Is there anything you want to see in particular?" I asked him. I was standing in the kitchen while we talked on the phone.

"You choose," he said.

The kitchen countertop in my apartment was made of white Formica that bubbled up at the seam where one piece of Formica butted up against another. I ran my fingers over the rough seam.

I didn't know how to choose a movie. Mike would judge me on my choice, of course. Even if he wouldn't say anything, I'd know in the way he'd react. If I suggested we see *Terminator 2*, he'd grunt the way our father—our own Archie Bunker—grunted when, as kids, we watched *All in the Family*, and his grunt was meant to say, "What kind of crap is this?" Or, if I suggested we see *Thelma and Louise*, Mike might say, "Huh," in the way our mother used to do when one of us suggested that we have pancakes for dinner and she meant, "That's not a very good idea, is it?"

While I was trying to think of an appropriate movie for Mike and me to see, I took a butter knife out of a drawer and ran it along the seam in the countertop to clean out the food scraps that collected there.

I'd spent most of my life trying to impress Mike, thinking that if he gave me his blessing, I'd do okay. When I was a sophomore in high school, I told Mike that I wanted to be a doctor—I had no real desire to be a doctor, but thought he would see my choice as noble. Instead, he said, "Is that right?" He meant that I didn't have the intellect or the discipline to make it through medical school. He was right, of course.

Mike's dismissal of me wasn't just about me. He had dismissed the entire family the moment he moved away from Indianapolis. He was embarrassed to have been born in the Midwest into such a parochial family. He felt cheated that we weren't privileged or at least upper-middle class.

"How about *Prospero's Books*?" I suggested to Mike over the phone.

"Sure," he said. I heard him rattling the ice in his glass, shaking loose the last of his cocktail.

My parents were very proud of their children. They thought of us as smart and talented and handsome—even if we weren't rich or sophisticated, as Mike had wanted. When we walked into church on Sunday—my father leading the way, our mother bringing up the rear, and the eight of us children filing in between them more or less in birth order—other parishioners poked their children, wishing they were more like us, or so our parents taught us to believe. In our neighborhood, according to my mother, housewives swapped stories about our successes—the sports trophies we'd won, the colleges we attended, the career paths we were set on.

Eventually, my oldest brother Tony would become a chief financial officer and my younger brothers Eddy and Rob would become an engineer and a computer programmer, respectively. Mike, of course, became a lawyer working for Morgan Stanley, one of the leading financial companies in the world. (My other older brother Joe had a learning disability, so we didn't expect much from him. My youngest brother Pat settled on a respectable career as a grade school principal. My sister Marie became a housewife, as was expected. When her kids were old enough to go to school, she received her master's in accounting, like my father had when I was a teenager.)

I was nothing like my brothers. While they played on the best Little League teams and won MVP awards, I was placed on the team sponsored by our local waste company—Mr. Removal. I tried as hard as I could to catch fly balls in the outfield and earn a decent batting average. But I did neither. My father watched one or two of my games, but he was more interested in the baseball games that Tony and Eddy and Rob (and even Mike) played in. Occasionally, my father would give me advice, the same advice my coaches gave me: "Keep your eye on the ball," "Squeeze your mitt to catch the ball," "Don't close your eyes." The advice didn't do any good. I lasted one season in Little League before quitting.

Instead, I was a boy who read alone in my room and sat by myself at the dining room table, carefully filling in the spaces of a Paint-by-Number set. I spent most of my childhood alone, listening to Mozart in my father's den, or teaching myself to knit in my mother's sewing room.

From their successes in summer sport's leagues, Tony went on to become an All-American athlete, while Eddy and Rob, and even

Mike, played on varsity squads. Their circle of friends expanded from the kids in our neighborhood to teammates who lived in gated communities in the wealthier suburbs to the north of the city, to college roommates from across the country and around the world. At the same time, I was withdrawing into myself, resisting my mother's call for me to go outside and play with my brothers. I avoided making eye contact with kids at school. I refused to take the advice of my teachers that I join the debate club or the student government association. When given a choice, I always chose solitude.

I felt as if I was a boy who had nothing in common with other boys, especially my brothers. This was true even of my relationship with Mike, who shared the same athletic enthusiasm and level of social engagement as my other brothers.

Looking back, I want to say that the difference I felt came from being gay; although, I also felt different from boys even before I knew that I was gay. Even though Mike was also gay, I never had the sense that he felt as different and as lonely as I had growing up. There was something else that separated me from other boys. I thought I was far more sensitive than they were, certainly more so than Mike was. I cried too easily when my brothers teased me, even though they teased each other—including Mike—just as harshly. I felt rejection more sharply, when my brothers were asked over to friends' houses for sleepovers and I was not.

Mike set the standard by which the teachers in our school judged me. Mike was popular—he was prom king and senior class president. He was a straight-A student. By the time I was a freshman in high school, he'd gone off to Notre Dame on a scholarship. I was not popular or smart—at least not in the way that counted. I disappointed my teachers, who thought that I'd perform as well as Mike. I was a B student.

Perhaps Mike's achievements were his way of overcompensating for feeling as abnormal as I felt—if, that is, he felt abnormal. If he did, I never saw it in him. Mike was cocky and self-assured. He seemed to be unfaltering in his belief that he could achieve anything. I never felt that way.

Instead, I learned to live in the shadows. In school, I slunk down in my desk when roll was called, and sat in the back of the auditorium during assembly. I kept my head down when I walked through the halls. I tried to make myself invisible, the unseen boy who'd never be missed if I simply disappeared.

I wanted to disappear. I wanted to opt out of life.

The first time I thought about dying was as a freshman in high school. I had a vague sense that I would never see my twenty-first birthday. I hadn't yet thought about killing myself, only that I couldn't go on year after year feeling as lonely as I felt. If someone was capable of dying of loneliness, I thought, I was a prime candidate, as if loneliness were a fatal disease that I was susceptible to.

Each year, my thoughts of dying became more concrete. I thought about what it would take to drown myself—how does one take in a breath of water?—or if the clothes bar in my closet were strong enough to hang myself from. I tried to imagine falling to my death from one of the tall buildings downtown, wondering what last thoughts I might have or if in such circumstances the mind is in too much shock to process thoughts.

I did try to make friends in high school, but I was so socially inept that these attempts always ended in disaster. When I was a junior, a guy in my class—Trevor—invited me to a party at his house when his parents had gone on vacation. I was excited to have been invited. I got blind drunk at that party and threw up first in the kitchen, and then in the living room, and finally in his parents' bedroom. I was so filled with shame that I jumped out of his parents' bedroom window and ran to my car rather than have to face Trevor and my classmates—or help clean up my mess. For the rest of junior year, I was known as the loser who'd gotten Trevor in serious trouble when his parents returned from vacation and knew what had happened from the smell the minute they walked into the house.

In the last semester of my senior year, my suicidal thoughts turned more serious. Over spring break—when my classmates were in Florida—I decided to kill myself.

After school on that Friday before spring break, I drove to a 7–11 and bought a pack of sleeping pills. I brought them home. The house was quiet. My mother and father were at work. My younger brothers—Eddy, Rob, and Pat—were at their after-school activities. My sister Marie and my older brothers Mike and Tony were off at college, while my other older brother Joe was at his vocational training classes. I took a glass of water from the kitchen and carried it up to my room with the sleeping pills. I locked my bedroom door. I took off my shoes. I poured the sleeping pills into my hand—the pack was small; there were only a half-dozen pills. I swallowed them. I lay down and slept for the next fifteen hours. I was disappointed when I woke up the next morning. My mother thought that I was simply tired and needed to sleep; my father hadn't noticed; and my three younger brothers didn't care.

A few weeks later, I was walking by the entrance to the high school gym, which doubled as our school's theater. There, on a bulletin board near the entrance, I saw a flyer announcing auditions for the Indianapolis Summer Shakespeare Festival.

I stopped, found myself studying a photo of actors on a stage in a local park in front of a crowd of people sitting on the lawn. At center stage was a woman, who was dressed in period costume. Her right hand was extended dramatically in front of her while her feet were firmly planted on the stage. Behind her were a group of actors in similar costumes. Everyone in the photo had their eyes fixed on the woman. She looked invincible.

I didn't know anything about Shakespeare other than what my high school English teacher, Mr. Stuart, had taught me. Mr. Stuart was strange. A small, round man with thinning hair and a red complexion, he looked as if he were always blushing. He wore flowery cologne that filled the classroom. He spoke with a faux British accent that was crisp and tight as if he had lockjaw. Most of my classmates made fun of him, but I liked him. By the time I had Mr. Stuart as a teacher, I knew that I was gay, and thought that he might be as well, although I never found out if he was or not.

When he taught us *Romeo and Juliet*, Mr. Stuart weaved up and down the rows of seats, making big gestures with his left hand while he read out the lines of the play from a large volume of Shakespeare that he held in his right. He seemed completely captivated by the play, even as most of us—including me—had no idea what he was saying.

Looking at that woman standing so resolutely in the flyer for the Indianapolis Summer Shakespeare Festival, I thought that just being next to someone like her might help me survive.

In early April of my senior year in 1981—when my classmates were getting excited for the prom—I drove over to a local church where auditions for *A Midsummer's Night Dream* and *Macbeth* were being held in the basement.

I was nervous when I got out of the car, walking slowly toward the entrance. I opened the door and walked in. I stood at the top of the stairs and listened for a while. I didn't understand the words being said, but I liked listening to them, as if that basement held a different world from the one I lived in.

When I walked down the stairs, I saw rows of metal chairs set up in the back half of the room, and a card table at the other end. Standing in front of the card table was the woman from the flyer. Tall and solid with a voice that boomed around the church basement, she was even more impressive in person. When I entered, she was giving instructions to a fat man who stood in the empty space between the table and the row of chairs.

"He's not a fool," she said to the fat man. "He's earnest in what he's saying. If you play him like a fool, it won't work. You have to play it honestly."

The fat man nodded, paused for a minute, and then began his audition again. I didn't know then what scene he was playing—it was Bottom and Titania's scene from Act 3 of *A Midsummer's Night Dream*—but I was mesmerized by the command and confidence that came with her voice, and the way her voice seemed to seduce the fat man.

I quietly slipped into the back row as the woman stopped the fat man, gave him another note, and he began the scene again.

The woman—her name was Camille—was a cofounder of the Indianapolis Summer Shakespeare Festival, and its lead actress. Her husband, Roger, was the other cofounder and its director. He was lumpy and unkempt, and continually stood up from behind the table, walked to the nearest wall, and then returned to his seat while the fat man was auditioning. Roger had a tendency to rub his fingertips together as if were rolling pebbles between them.

I hadn't thought what it meant to audition for a play. I hadn't imagined that I'd be asked to stand in front of a room of people and recite lines that I'd never read. I should've left, but I was too mesmerized by Camille to leave. I suppose it was the authority in her voice.

One after the other, the people who'd come to audition stood in front of Camille as she read out the counterpart to their audition pieces. When everyone had finished, Camille looked at me. I slid down low in my seat, but she didn't take her eyes off of me. She motioned for me to come forward like a revival-tent preacher who could spot a sinner a mile away. I felt compelled to stand in that empty space between her and everyone else. I kept my eyes down until she told me to look at her. I blushed when I did.

"Have you ever acted in a play before?" she asked me.

I shook my head. Up close, I could see the fine hairs at her temples—she had brownish-blonde hair that she kept tied up loosely in a bun—and her thick eyebrows that she kept plucked around the edges.

She handed me her copy of the play.

"Read here," she said, pointing to a line on the page. Her fingernails were cut short and painted maroon or dark blue—I can't remember which. I do remember being surprised that her nails were painted, thinking that she was too tough to care about cosmetics.

I looked at her, not completely understanding what she'd asked me to do.

"Just that one line," she said, tapping her finger on the page.

I took the playbook, looked at the line she'd pointed to, and then said it out loud.

"What's your will?"

It was Mustardseed's line. He was one of the fairies that attended Titania, the Queen of the Fairies.

When I spoke the line, I tried to imitate Mr. Stuart's faux British accent but I ended up sounding as if I'd been born somewhere in the deep South.

From the folding chairs, I heard giggles. I looked up at Camille to see if she was laughing at me as well. She held her face steady: her lips parted slightly and her eyes relaxed.

My hands were shaking and the playbook fluttered in them. Camille took my wrists to steady my hands.

"Do it again," Camille said to me. She'd lowered her voice so that only I could hear what she was saying. "But this time use your regular voice. As if you've just opened the door and are greeting someone you know."

Behind Camille, I could see Roger rubbing his fingertips together and looking over his notes on the people who'd auditioned.

"Keep your eyes on me," Camille said, looking at me steadily.

I repeated the line in the way Camille had told me without looking away from her.

"Good," she said. "That wasn't so difficult, was it?"

It wasn't, I thought.

She told me that I could come back.

Every day after school, I returned to the church basement and rehearsed with the other actors. The same company of players was cast in both plays: the fat man played Bottom and Macbeth; Camille played Titania and Lady Macbeth; and I played Mustardseed and a messenger.

Because I had so few lines, I spent most of my time in rehearsal watching Camille move around the practice stage and listening to her voice. After a while, her speeches became familiar to me and I began to understand the words she was speaking. In Mr. Stuart's class, Shakespeare was just a garbled string of words. Listening to Camille, Shakespeare became poetry that over time I understood.

Even though I was a peripheral character in these plays, I felt as if I belonged to the world the other actors where creating, a world in which I could be a fairy worshipping at the foot of a queen, or a page serving a noble house, even if that house was full of drama and envy and doom. I thought that if it were possible to inhabit new worlds created by the language of Shakespeare, then perhaps someday I could create a completely different kind of world than the one I'd been living in, one in which I'd been so desperate to escape that I was willing to kill myself. In those weeks and months of rehearsals, I began to gain a glimpse of what was possible, when before I never liked to think of the future.

That May, I graduated from high school. In July, I stood on the stage I'd seen in the photo on the flyer. I was in the background in both *A Midsummer Night's Dream* and *Macbeth*, but still I felt a part of the company. When the audience applauded for them—for Camille mostly—I felt that they were applauding for me, too. It felt as if I belonged in this strange world that I'd found.

My mother and father had come to see the plays—none of my brothers nor my sister did. Afterward, my father said that he had a hard time understanding what was going on in the plays. My mother said that I did well, even if she too couldn't figure out the plots.

I went off to college in the fall after the shows had closed. I was not yet strong or bold enough to resist my father's insistence that I major in accounting. However, I returned every summer to play various minor parts in all the major plays the Indianapolis Summer Shakespeare Festival staged—a captain telling Hamlet of Fortinbras's campaign, a boy bringing Benedick his book, a plebian in the crowd listening to Antony praise Caesar. And every summer I felt as if I were simultaneously moving away from my family and into a different kind of life where I might find kinship that mattered to me, and that would accept me without preconditions.

While Shakespeare's plays gave me a sense of the imaginary, being part of the company also introduced me to a gay community that I didn't know existed. Many of the actors who rotated through the festival were gay, and while I never became a core part of their group—I was still too shy and afraid to assert myself—I took comfort in knowing that there was another clan besides my family that I could belong to.

When I moved to D.C., I did belong to the gay community there. I hung out with a small group of friends at JR's, and occasionally met them for brunch at restaurants in DuPont Circle, and sometimes went with them to gay clubs in the southeast quadrant of the city. Belonging to the gay community allowed me to build the kind of life I wanted to live, and not the life my family expected me to live.

I suppose that I was trying to achieve the same kind of transformation that Mike was seeking. While he was living in New York and telling people that he was an only child with a trust fund, I was living in D.C. as part of a community that valued art and the theater and independent film—so unlike my family who preferred entertainment that was easy to understand and easy to put aside. My family read Tom Clancy novels and watched Disney movies. They hung Thomas Kinkade paintings on their walls and filled their homes with Hallmark tchotchke. They never stepped foot in a museum or an art gallery or an exhibition.

I made plans to meet Mike in front of the KB Janus Theater on Connecticut Avenue in Washington, D.C., for the 4:45 showing of *Prospero's Books*. I'd wanted to see Peter Greenaway's new movie the moment I read the review in the *Washington Post*. The reviewer, Hal Hinson, called it "a true feast for the eye," but "also a chore to sit through—off-puttingly tedious and obscure." The movie was Greenaway's interpretation of Shakespeare's *The Tempest*, which I knew very well from playing a sprite in the Indianapolis Summer Shakespeare Festival production where my lines included "Bow wow," and "Ding Dong, bell." Hinson wrote, however, that *Prospero's Books* was so loosely fashioned after the play that the movie was "impenetrable."

If I wanted to impress Mike with my choice of movies, I thought that *Prospero's Books* would be familiar enough to me so that I'd get the basic plot, and intellectual enough for Mike's ego. I thought that at the very least I could fake a conversation about the movie over dinner.

Mike was late, of course. I paced in front of the theater with the tickets in my hand, wondering if I shouldn't just go in and watch the movie by myself. But I was excited to see Mike, as I'd always been excited to see him, even if he didn't seem to care for me one way or the other most of the time.

Finally, Mike walked casually up to the theater.

"Oh, hey," he said as if we hadn't made plans for the evening, and we'd just happened to bump into each other.

He wore a pair of jeans with a crease down the front of each leg from having been ironed, brown desert boots, and a pea coat.

"You're late," I said, sounding shrill.

We stood looking at each other for a few seconds. I took a step toward him to give him a hug, but he took a step back from me as if I were going to attack him. His reaction to my gesture confused me—why would I attack him? I thought. I took a step back to show him that I didn't mean any harm.

Once, after I'd earned a Citizenship badge during a ceremony for the local Boy Scout club that I briefly belonged to—I'd helped an elderly woman in our neighborhood with her groceries to earn the award—I was so proud of myself that I went to hug my father. In front of all the other fathers who'd gathered to watch their sons receive badges—more important ones like Hunting and Archery and Fire Safety—my father stood with his hands down at his side while I wrapped myself around his waist. After a few seconds, he pushed me away and sat down without saying a word. On the car ride home, my father told me that I needed to learn to control my emotional outbursts.

In front of the KB Janus, Mike looked at me in a similar way that my father had looked at me after the Boy Scout ceremony. Mike's brows were furrowed and his lips were pursed. He buttoned the top button of his pea coat as if he suddenly felt a chill.

Mike and I settled on a firm handshake.

I tried to hurry him into the theater, but he took his time. He stopped at the concession stand and bought popcorn and a soda. He looked at the posters for the movies playing in the other theaters.

"Hey, this one looks good," he said, pointing to the handsome young man in the poster for the movie *Europa, Europa*.

"Let's go," I said impatiently.

He lingered a few minutes and flirted with the boy who collected tickets.

The KB Janus was a terrible place to watch a movie. We used to refer to it as the "Heinous Janus." There were three theaters, and they were all small, more like large living rooms than movie theaters. The seats were crammed too close together so that it was impossible to sit next to someone without your body touching the body next to you. But it was an "art house," and I thought Mike would appreciate it. He didn't.

When I finally got Mike into the theater, we sat in the back. I gave him the aisle seat and sat next to him.

"This theater is pretty crappy," Mike said out loud. The guy sitting a few seats in front of us turned around and hushed Mike. He gave the guy the finger.

I looked at Mike, shrugged my shoulders and shook my head to indicate my confusion over his behavior. He ignored me.

When the movie started, the opening scenes were strange. In what appears to be a bathhouse, John Gielgud—who plays Prospero—is standing naked waist deep in a pool while overhead a boy—the sprite, Ariel—swings as he's peeing into the pool. In front of Gielgud is a desk that shields our view of his genitals. Behind Gielgud are bookcases crammed with books that overwhelm the space. (Throughout the movie, each frame is filled with books and papers and scenery so that the viewer feels as if he's drowning.) On the desk in front of Gielgud there is a stack of parchment and an inkwell. Gielgud dips a quill into the inkwell, and begins to scratch out the story of how he was betrayed by his brother Antonio, who took Prospero's throne as the Duke of Milan.

"Why is that kid peeing in the pool?" Mike asked out loud. He wasn't asking me but rather himself. He crunched loudly on his popcorn.

The boy, like all of the creatures on this haunted island—where Prospero and his only child Miranda have been living since Antonio cast them out onto the sea and expected them to drown—are wild and uncivilized. What wild creature wouldn't pee in a body of water, I asked myself? What kid hasn't peed in a swimming pool just because he had to pee and he happened to be in a pool?

Obviously, Mike knew nothing about Peter Greenaway—the director of the disturbingly bloody movie *The Cook, The Thief, His Wife & Her Lover*—nor had Mike read the *Post*'s review of *Prospero's Books*. It seemed to me from the opening scenes that Mike wasn't even going to try to understand the movie. Perhaps, like the rest of my brothers, ambiguity angered Mike. As accountants and engineers and computer programmers and lawyers, Mike and my brothers (and my father) insisted on viewing the world in black and white. They found uncertainty threatening.

When Gielgud emerges from the pool and his servants wrap him in a traditional Italian Renaissance robe that befits a Duke—a robe made of heavily embossed deep red fabric—Gielgud is attended by a troupe of naked dancers who process around the oversaturated bathhouse in exaggerated modern dance moves—legs projected at stiff angles, bodies jerking back and forth from the hip, hands held sharply away from the body.

I looked over at Mike to see how he was reacting to these stylized attendants. He was staring quietly at the naked men on screen. I smiled. At least, I thought, the sight of so many cocks had shut him up for the moment. For all his intellect and bravado, Mike seemed easily tamed by the sight of nakedness. He was ashamed, perhaps, to be sitting next to his younger gay brother and forced to see what I was seeing, confronted with our shared desire for men but not wanting to acknowledge our commonality.

When the character of Caliban came on screen, however, Mike couldn't help himself. Caliban looked like a tortured animal that had been living in squalor.

"That's fucking gross," Mike said out loud.

The man who was sitting in front of us got up from this seat, stared at Mike in an attempt to intimidate him—although Mike wasn't intimidated—and then left the theater in a huff.

The actor who played Caliban—Michael Clark, a famous dancer trained at the Royal Ballet School in London—was tall and lean. In the movie, he wears a corset that tightly encases his torso and wraps between his legs like a dancer's belt, but one in which the crotch has been cut out. The actor's genitals are bundled tightly together with red gauze like a slave in an S/M relationship. He moves exquisitely around the island; his legs and arms extending from one rocky outcropping to the next; his tight torso twisting in the same fashion as a rushing stream that moves through a gorge; his head thrown back in ecstatic celebration of the overgrown wilderness.

I was attracted to this Caliban. He was as at once beautiful and dangerous, attractive and repulsive. Whenever Caliban came on the screen, I turned my body away from Mike so that he couldn't see my erection.

In *The Tempest*, Prospero causes Antonio and his court to be shipwrecked on the island so that Prospero can seek his revenge. In Greenaway's movie, these men are dressed in highly stylized Renaissance costumes with large Elizabethan collars and oversized hats with ridiculous plumage and large codpieces and platform shoes that the actors looked uncomfortable walking in. Everything in Greenaway's movie is exaggerated to capture the exotic nature of the play, and the complex relationship between brothers and rivals and cultures.

I thought that if Mike couldn't understand the boy peeing in the pool or the naked attendants or the erotic Caliban, that surely he could understand the fraught relationship between brothers—between Prospero and Antonio. Wasn't that what defined our relationship to our brothers, or even the relationship between us? I thought. But as with the rest of the film, Mike dismissed these characters with a loud "Jesus!" because they appeared to him to be fools. Ridiculous looking men who couldn't be taken seriously.

Throughout *Prospero's Books*, we see Gielgud writing out the story of his exile and his desire to seek revenge. We see, that is, the text of Shakespeare's play *The Tempest* being created by the main character of the play. I thought this point of Greenaway's movie was brilliant. I'd understood that the actors in the Indianapolis Summer Shakespeare Festival had created their own worlds in which they inhabited new versions of themselves. I saw in *Prospero's Books* characters writing their own stories, creating their own realities, coming up with their own conclusions. It was the first time that I had a sense of what a writer could create, as opposed to what an actor could inhabit. I understood, in other words, the possibility of creating a new world for myself through writing, one in which I could choose to seek revenge on a family of brothers, who I felt had abandoned me, or to forgive them and move on.

At the end of *The Tempest* and *Prospero's Books*, rather than take his revenge on his brother, Prospero decides to forgive him, as Antonio agrees to restore Prospero to his rightful place as the Duke of Milan.

What Mike saw as stupid in the movie, I saw as magnificent. What he found confusing, I found illuminating. When he complained that the plot made no sense, I was amazed at the way Greenaway had taken a play about a duke taking revenge on his usurping brother, and turned it into a movie about writing.

I sat in the KB Janus and tried not to listen to Mike's complaints. Instead, I concentrated on the language in the movie the way I'd done with Camille. I understood the strangeness of the place Prospero had been exile to—I'd felt the same way growing up in my family. I felt Prospero's need to rewrite the world in order to make sense of it. I knew what it was to be lonely and to feel as if your family had abandoned you. I, too, had grown bitter and vengeful.

I looked up to Mike, but listening to him complain in the KB Janus—and shoving fistfuls of popcorn into his mouth—I was disheartened. He was no better than my other brothers, I thought. If they were sitting next to me watching the same movie, they would have behaved in the same way Mike had.

I wanted Mike to be something different, something better than the rest of my brothers. I wanted him to be kinder and more understanding. I wanted him to be empathetic, to have the capacity to understand the kind of life I'd lived as a child—that lonely childhood—and the desperation I'd felt when I'd wanted to kill myself. I wanted Mike to be all the family I'd ever want or need.

When he expressed his disgust at the creature of Caliban, I wanted to punch Mike and tell him to grow up. I didn't, though. I let him behave like an ass and tried to pretend I didn't know him.

When the movie was over, Mike bolted out of the theater while I stayed and watched the credits roll. I wanted to feel happy that I understood the movie when Mike clearly hadn't. For my entire life, I'd thought that Mike was smarter than me in every way. But he knew nothing about art and literature. He was a child with a petulant mind who didn't want to admit his ignorance.

When the last credit rolled, I slowly walked out of the theater. Mike was waiting on the sidewalk, pacing back and forth as if he couldn't wait to get away from the theater, as if it had been the sight of some trauma he couldn't endure.

"What was that shit about?" Mike asked when he saw me. He threw his hands up in the air.

"Did you have to talk throughout the movie?" I asked, moving past him and down the block. He followed me. He was never the one to follow behind. That was my role.

"Come on," he said when he caught up with me. "That was a piece of shit." He moved in front of me and tried to block me from going forward. I sidestepped him and continued down the block.

"I liked it," I said calmly. I was never calm around Mike. I was always anxious, hoping that he'd give me the attention I'd always wanted from him. I didn't care about attracting his attention after seeing *Prospero's Books*, however.

"No, really," he said when I didn't agree with him. "You liked that?"

"Yes," I said.

I was walking up Connecticut Avenue to R Street. I'd planned to take Mike to an Italian restaurant on Sixteenth Street for dinner, and then over to JR's for drinks afterward. Whether or not he still wanted to have dinner with me, I was going to the restaurant and JR's. I didn't mind eating alone, or drinking alone. I'd done it a dozen times before.

"Then tell me why," Mike asked, his voice was calmer and more regulated, the way I'd always known it to be from a man who, I thought, had an abundance of self-confidence.

"Do you really want to know?" I asked. "Or do you just want to make fun of me?"

"I want to know," he said. "Honestly."

As we turned onto R Street, I rehearsed the plot of *The Tempest* with Mike.

"So it's a family drama," Mike joked.

"I suppose it is," I said, smiling.

"But what was *that*?" Mike asked, referring to Greenaway's adaption of *The Tempest*.

"That," I said, "was a meditation on writing."

When I was eight years old, I had a vague notion that I wanted to be a writer. Much like acting, I didn't know anything about writing. All that I had was the desire to write.

In my sister's bedroom, I began to write a story in one of my school notebooks. I started with a description of a boy—who looked unsurprisingly like me—and of a forest, which resembled the woods that lay at the end of our street. When it was time to move the boy into the forest and set off on his adventure, however, I didn't have the skill to do this. I could see the boy walking down the street, entering the forest, and hunting for raspberries but I couldn't figure out how to organize my thoughts into these actions. I had no experience in translating the images in my head into words on a page. Soon, I became frustrated and tore up the paper.

Watching *Prospero's Books*, I felt as if what I was seeing on screen resembled what I'd experienced as an eight-year-old boy: the workings of a chaotic and creative mind. In the movie, however, Prospero is capable of filtering and organizing his thoughts into a story that had a plot, even if that plot wasn't crystal clear.

"I want to be a writer," I said to Mike as we turned onto Sixteenth Street.

I don't know why I said this to him in that moment. My family thought that art was a joke made by people too stupid to making a real living, or a hobby for bored housewives. If they knew that I wanted to be a writer, I reasoned, they'd laugh at me and call me foolish. Perhaps after seeing *Prospero's Books* with Mike and feeling just then that he held less sway over my life, I didn't care whether or not Mike approved of what I wanted to do.

"I'd like to have a writer as a brother," he said simply.

I stopped on the sidewalk in front of the restaurant and looked at him. I couldn't tell if he was being serious or not. I thought that he was being serious.

It was the first time that I'd heard words of encouragement from him, from any of my brothers. At that moment, it felt as if I'd finally stepped out of the shadows of my childhood. It seemed as if Mike had recognized me as an individual rather than as a younger brother. I imagined that one day—when I had published a book—Mike might be proud of me, of introducing me to his friends as a published author. "The talented one in the family," I imagined him saying. "The one who outshines us all."

It turned out, however, that Mike's desire to have a writer as a brother was no more important to him than having a share on Fire Island, or an apartment in Chelsea, or the ability to spend as much money as he wanted on an expensive dinner. He'd spent his life accumulating the trappings of a sophisticated life in an attempt to escape his past as a Midwestern boy growing up in an unremarkable middle-class family. Having a writer as a brother was just one more eccentricity he wanted around him, until the façade on his fake life slipped away and he was left with nothing.

Holiday Inn

The summer before he died, Mike and I returned to Indianapolis to visit our family. (David didn't come with me. My family was too much to bear most of the time.) Mike and I spent the weekend with the rest of our family at my parents' summerhouse on Lake Cordry, a man-made lake forty miles south of Indianapolis.

There was nothing special about the lake house. It was the second to last house built on a gravel road that dead-ended in one of the lake's coves. A kitchen, bedroom, bathroom, dining room, and living room were on the top level. Two bedrooms, a bathroom, and a TV room were on the lower level. The walls were covered in wood paneling and there was sculpted carpeting throughout. My parents had filled the house with secondhand furniture they'd bought at garage sales—enormous overstuffed couches and broken La-Z-Boy chairs that couldn't pop out their footrests and squat, wooden tables that looked immovable. The house smelled lived in and mildewed.

The house was packed with family: our siblings, their spouses, and our ten nieces and nephews. There was nowhere Mike or I could go to get away. Our family was everywhere—running up and down the stairs, raiding the refrigerator, crowding into the TV room to watch whatever sports program was playing. We were drowning in family.

While the house felt small and claustrophobic with all those people, the backyard was expansive. A weedy lawn sloped down from the house all the way to a dock that jutted out into the cove.

When they weren't invading the house, our nieces and nephews played down by the water. The kids liked to jump off the dock, holding cannonball contests to see who could make the biggest splash. A rope hung from a large oak tree along the edge of the cove, and they swung out on that rope and dropped into the water. Next to the dock, one of my brothers had made a small beach with sand he'd trucked in from a local stone yard. The littlest of the kids played on the beach where their mothers—our sisters-in-law—could keep an eye on them. My father had a pontoon boat tied to the dock that he took out periodically during the day so that the kids could go to the middle of the lake and swim out where the water was deeper and colder.

Late that Saturday morning, Mike and I sat on the back deck drinking coffee and watching our nieces and nephews play. Our brothers were scattered about doing yard work. Their wives were looking after the kids. My mother and sister were in the kitchen cleaning up the breakfast dishes. My father was in the TV room watching a golf tournament.

At one point, my oldest nephew Ben jumped off the dock and landed on his younger cousin Amy. Ben's father—my oldest brother Tony—yelled at Ben the way my father used to yell at Tony when he was a kid. My sister Marie's younger daughter, Lynn, stubbed her toe racing up the concrete stairs and screamed at the top of her lungs until Marie swooped her up and carried her into the house to clean and bandage Lynn's wound.

There was a constant flurry of activity and noise that Mike and I weren't used to. We stayed put on the back porch drinking our coffee and keeping our distance.

"Aren't you glad we're not like them?" Mike asked, gesturing to our brothers and their hordes of children.

"Definitely," I said.

"I'd go fucking mad," Mike said.

"I suppose you'd get used to it."

"I doubt it," he said.

At one point, our youngest brother Pat passed us on the back porch as he was heading into the house to get something for one of his kids.

"Look at you two," Pat said. "Confirmed bachelors without a care in the world."

Mike and I raised our coffee mugs in salute.

"Confirmed bachelors," Mike said with a sneer after Pat went into the house.

"Who uses that phrase anymore?" I asked. Besides, I thought, David and I were just as much of a couple, only one that my family didn't recognize.

Mike shrugged his shoulders.

Our family never could figure out how to place Mike and me into their idea of what a good life was supposed to be. Mike and I were the family outliers. Two grown men without wives or children, without—they assumed—any real purpose in life.

Later in the afternoon, Mike and I put on our swimsuits. I wore a pair of green Vilebrequin swim trunks with slices of oranges and lemons printed on them. Mike wore a crotch-hugging Speedo. He had the same hairy chest and legs that I did. He also had a belly that protruded slightly—the same protruding belly that I had, one that would, as I grew older, turn into our father's beer gut.

"Really?" I said to Mike when he came out of the bedroom in his Speedo.

"What?" he asked.

"Do you think we're on Fire Island?"

Mike never missed an opportunity to provoke a reaction from our family. When we walked out of the house and down to the dock, he dared any of our brothers to comment on his Speedo. They didn't, though I thought I heard Pat chuckle.

Our nieces and nephews didn't care what kind of swimsuits we wore. They were just happy to have their absent uncles to play with.

For a little while, Mike and I played with our nieces and nephews—doing cannonballs and swinging off the tree rope and splashing around in the cove. But they quickly grew tired of us as kids so easily grow tired of adults. Then Mike and I swam out to the mouth of the cove where it opened up to the rest of the lake. We stopped there and treaded water for a while.

"You know," Mike said at one point, "sooner or later we're going to have to forgive him."

The water out near the opening of the cove was colder than the water near the dock. A warm current from the cove would wash over our feet. We'd stop treading water and sink down into that warm current, before bobbing back up to the surface and continuing to tread water.

I had no intention of forgiving our father, and I couldn't understand why Mike insisted then that we had to forgive him.

"Why?" I asked Mike.

"We can't hate him forever," he said.

"Yes, we can," I said.

Before then, I didn't realize that my animosity toward my father was greater than Mike's. He was willing to forgive my father, while forgiveness had never crossed my mind. I couldn't remember a time when I liked my father, perhaps because by the time I was born he was busy trying to provide for our ever-growing family and was, for the most part, absent from my life. He was always working. No matter how noble my father's intentions were, for a kid, an absent father is just an absent father.

In his suicide note, Mike wrote, "I wish I were more like you dad who can attribute it all to God's will & get on with it. I think God is all that matters as well as family." This line made no sense to me when I first read Mike's note in the 18th Police Precinct in Manhattan. It wasn't until later that I remembered treading water on Lake Cordry and Mike insisting that we had to forgive our father. I guess he had forgiven my father by the time Mike killed himself. I still haven't.

I suppose that when Mike and I were sitting on that back porch and celebrating our confirmed bachelorhoods, Mike wasn't being honest. I thought that Mike and I had a special bond because we were not like our brothers. They believed that God and family were all that mattered. Perhaps, at the moment of his death, Mike looked back at that familial scene down at the lake house and saw a storied life that he imagined might've made him happy. That summer weekend at Lake Cordry, I saw a family I no longer wanted to be a part of, while perhaps Mike saw a family that once accepted him but then had pushed him away.

I don't remember what grade I was in when I first read Edith Wharton's novel *The House of Mirth*. I only remember that it struck me in a different way than it struck my classmates. For them, the novel was a study in nineteenth-century manners, just as our teacher had told us: the role of women in society, the focus on traditional marriage, the anxiety over financial security. But for me, there was something more personal about it. The first time I read the novel, I didn't get all the plot details—which rich wife was having an affair with which young bachelor; who inherited whose money and who didn't; the social machinations of the Manhattan elite. What struck me were the feelings I had for the novel's protagonist, Lily Bart. Her story was easy to follow. She was a single woman in a world that only cared about money and marriage, and she had neither. She was vulnerable to the dictates of power and the desires of greedy men.

Lily was born into a wealthy family, but her father lost their fortune in a business venture. After her parents died, Lily was left to fend for herself. Now, at twenty-nine years old, Lily knows that she must marry soon if she is to retain her social status.

In the first scene of the novel, Lily is having tea with Lawrence Selden—a confirmed bachelor and Lily's long-term friend—in his apartment. Lily is aware that her society would frown on a single woman being alone in a man's apartment. But, as Selden notices, there's a kind of wildness in Lily that is difficult for her to constrain. She is "a captured dryad subdued to the conventions of the drawing-room."

One of Lily's potential suitors—Sim Rosedale—catches Lily coming out of Selden's apartment building. Rosedale asks Lily what she is doing there, and Lily lies and says that she's visiting her dressmaker. She regrets this lie and knows that it will come back to haunt her. Wharton writes:

Why must a girl pay so dearly for her least escape from routine? Why could one never do a natural thing without having to screen it behind a structure of artifice? She had yielded to a passing impulse in going to Lawrence Selden's rooms, and it was so seldom that she could allow herself the luxury of an impulse! This one, at any rate, was going to cost her rather more than she could afford. She was vexed to see that, in spite of so many years of vigilance, she had blundered.

It was this predicament that first drew me to Lily and to *The House of Mirth*. Both the constant pressure to marry and the need she felt to hide behind a "structure of artifice." Isn't this what every gay man of a certain age felt growing up? Isn't this the same pressure and need we've felt? It was for me, at least.

From the peer pressure in middle school and high school to always have a girlfriend, and the teasing from my brothers about girls they assumed I had a crush on, to the family conversations around the dinner table about our future as married men giving my parents grandchildren, the pressure to be straight and to marry was everywhere. It was understood that I would follow the same path that my brothers were expected to follow, the same path my father and grandfather and generations of men had followed: get married and have children. I couldn't escape it, even though I knew that I would never marry and have children the way my brothers would—the way I assumed Mike would before I knew that he was gay.

To hide my sexuality, I dated girls who were boisterous and large and overly social. They drew all the attention so that no one saw me standing there awkwardly in their shadows.

My freshman year at Bishop Chatard High School, I became friends with Susan. She fit my criteria for a fake girlfriend. She was from a large Catholic family like mine. She was shorter than I was and had thick black hair and big breasts. She had a loud, high-pitched voice that filled the school's hallways.

Susan was kind to me. She put up with my moods and listened to my complaints about my family. I considered us to be close friends. She considered us to be dating, and hoped that one day we'd get married. She often talked about the number of kids she'd like to have—at least five—and the kind of house she'd like to live in—a colonial—and the size of our wedding—big enough so that all of her siblings and all of my siblings could stand at the altar with us.

After a spring dance in our sophomore year, we made out in my car on a side street not far from our high school. At one point, she thrust my hands under her bra so that I could feel her breasts. They felt like great mounds of uncooked dough rising in a warm kitchen. I kneaded them until she pulled my hands from under her bra. After our junior prom, she took me back to her house where we dry humped on the living room carpet after her parents went to bed. She grinded her crotch up against my tuxedo pants and moaned as if she were in ecstasy. I tried to match her enthusiasm, but there was nothing going on in my pants.

Making out with Susan was a strange, non-erotic experience for me. It felt more like a chore, like checking off an item on a list that would prove that I was straight: make out with a woman—check; touch her breasts—check; dry hump in her parents' house—check.

At the same time I was "dating" Susan, I was having sex with guys in dark parking lots and abandoned stretches of road and in mall bathrooms. The sex was rough and dangerous and messy. It was also electric and heart pounding. There was never a question of me getting it up or getting off with these guys.

The pressure to hide behind the artifice of being straight while worrying that someone would discover that I was gay was too much for me. I felt like I lived on the edge of an abyss, and if I made one false move I'd die.

If I thought that escaping high school would relieve the pressure to be straight, I was wrong. When I went to college the pressure increased. My dorm-mates were always talking about the women they slept with and asking me about my sexual conquests. I hadn't had sex with a woman, so I had no way of answering their questions except with obvious lies. I felt threatened by these men, thinking that if they found out that I was gay, they'd harm me. To protect myself, I had sex with a woman—a friend of a friend that I met at a party. I don't remember her name. She took me back to her apartment. She was undressed before I was. Having sex with her felt as strange and unnatural to me as it might with a sea urchin.

As with Susan, there was nothing erotic about this sexual encounter; it was just another check on that list of heterosexuality that I still carried around in my head.

The pressure from my family to get married was relentless. By the time I was in college, my sister and older brother had already married and were having children. There was never a visit home when my family didn't ask about the women I was supposedly dating, and my marriage prospects. They assumed that once I graduated from college that I'd settle down and begin raising a family. Even when I moved away to Washington, D.C., after college and got a job selling shoes at Nordstrom, every phone call with my mother ended with questions of marriage and children until I stopped taking her calls, and she eventually stopped calling.

The pressure to marry didn't cease until my family found out that I was gay. Then I became a different kind of brother and son to them. One who lived outside of their circle of being husbands and fathers, of families creating more family. Throughout all ages. World without end. Amen!

After having read *The House of Mirth* the first time, I understood the structure of artifice that was built around Lily. I'd also felt the pressure of marriage and the need to live behind a façade. *The House of Mirth* wasn't just a Victorian novel of manners as it was to my teacher and my classmates; it was a confirmation that the pressures I felt when I was living in the closet were real and dangerous. That the game I felt I was forced to play in the conservative society in which I grew up had deadly consequences.

Mike had written his suicide note at a desk in room 2906 of the Holiday Inn Crowne Plaza in Times Square. He'd written the note on the hotel's stationery, using—I'm assuming—the complimentary pen that lay next to the pad of paper. As he wrote, he drank the bottle of NyQuil he'd brought with him, and then the vodka tonic he'd laced with pentobarbital. He'd fall off the chair and land on his back on the carpeted floor before he could finish the note. There was no time for him to sign off, to write, perhaps, "Love, Mike," or "Sincerely, Mike," or "Goodbye, Mike." Instead, his handwriting slipped and his last words became illegible.

Maybe he hadn't planned to write a note at all—most people who kill themselves don't. Maybe at the last minute he wanted to try to understand how he'd gotten to that hotel room and why death was his only option.

When I read his note, however, I didn't find any satisfying explanations, or any good reasons why he killed himself. I saw only excuses that didn't ring true, and strange references that seemed as if someone else had written the note, even though I knew Mike had written it. I could tell by his handwriting: the stiff peaks of the "M" in "Mom," the open and rounded "D" of "Dad." His handwriting was always precise and delicate, the way we were taught to write cursive by the nuns in our Catholic grade school. But then Mike wrote, "I loved you all so dearly," and I thought that the person who would have used such a phrase was not the brother I knew. "I loved you all so dearly" wasn't a phrase anyone in my family ever used. It wasn't even a phrase from the twentieth century but better suited to a nineteenth-century novel like *The House of Mirth*.

I want to believe that Mike held so much love for us that it overwhelmed him just at that moment when he was about to die. But I don't remember a time when I felt an abundance of love from him. Instead, my memories of Mike are filled with me wanting more from him than he could give: more attention and admiration and encouragement and support. I suppose he was too consumed with living his life behind his own structure of artifice to care much about me.

After Mike's funeral, my mother went back to New York to pack up his apartment. She also went downtown to his office to take the few personal items that were there: his framed diplomas from the University of Notre Dame and Duke University, a pad of stationery with his name embossed on it, and his nameplate. When Mike's colleagues met my mother, they were surprised to see her. They were equally surprised to learn that Mike had seven siblings. At Mike's funeral, his colleagues told me that Mike said he was an only child and that his parents had died when he was young. He was an orphan, he told his colleagues, and was forced to make it on his own. In the seven years that Mike had been living in New York, he was creating his own narrative and trying to occupy a story that wasn't his.

When he came home for visits, Mike tried to impose this fictive life on the rest of us. He assumed an air of superiority that the rest of us found comical. He acted as if he'd come to some grand estate where we'd play bridge all weekend while my brothers just wanted to watch football. My father tried to placate Mike. My father ran out every morning to find the *Times* so that Mike would have it at the breakfast table, as if my father were Mike's personal valet.

At Christmas and on birthdays, Mike gave ridiculous gifts that he'd bought on shopping sprees at Barney's. One year he gave my mother an Iittala vase embellished with colored glass leaves that would've looked fine in an Upper Eastside apartment, but which was out of place on the shelf next to the TV in my parents' suburban home. During dinner, Mike expected us to banter about as if we were at a soiree. He might say, "Nothing exemplifies the downfall of America like a Sunday afternoon dedicated to sports." No one would respond. We didn't know how to respond. We just sat there and pretended we hadn't heard him.

No sooner would he arrive home than my siblings counted the minutes until he left. Even my father grew tired of him after a while. (My mother, on the other hand, tried to hold on to him as long as she could.)

In his note, Mike wrote, "I hate all the pain this will cause you." I'm not sure my siblings felt much pain when Mike died. My sister Marie told me that when Mike moved away from home, it felt as if he'd died then. He wasn't part of Marie's day-to-day life, and so she wrote him off long before he actually died. I think my brothers did as well. Over the years, I've tried to adopt the attitude of my siblings, but obviously I've failed. I suppose this is true because I saw something good in Mike even when he was at his worst. Even when he lied to me or betrayed me, he was still my brother and I wasn't willing to let go of him.

Besides, I don't think Mike was really concerned with the pain his death would cause any of us. Rather, as he writes, "my only response can be that my own personal pain is just overwhelming." This is what people who commit suicide always say. I would've liked to have the chance to challenge his assumption. To engage in a debate—as he was so famous for doing with his family and friends—over the premise of his conclusion. To argue that rarely in life is there only one response to any given situation. After all, he could've checked himself into a hospital, or sought professional help, or—if he was really desperate—picked up the phone and called his brother.

The last time I saw Mike was at our brother Rob's wedding. Rob was the last of our brothers to marry. It was August. The un-air-conditioned church was stifling. The bride nearly fainted at the altar.

The day after the wedding, my mother, Mike, David, and I went down to the lake house. My father stayed back at the house in Indianapolis, and my other brothers had plans with their families.

It was late in the morning. My mother sat on the back porch drinking coffee. Mike, David, and I sat at the edge of the dock with our feet in the water. Mike wore his Speedo. David and I wore our Vilebrequins—David's swim trunks were blue with red chili peppers printed on them. It was going to be a hot day.

I don't remember the conversation we had. It probably had something to do with the family and being back in Indiana. But at one point Mike asked me, "If you were going to kill yourself, how would you do it?"

David was shocked by Mike's question. No one in David's family would ever ask such a question. As kids, however, my brothers and I used to play this game of what-if all the time. "What if you were going to murder someone? How would you do it without getting caught?" or "What if you were going to rob a bank? How would you get away with it?" They were just hypothetical questions that none of us took seriously.

"I'd OD," I said to Mike. "I'd take enough pills so that I was sure I wouldn't wake up."

I had tried to kill myself by taking sleeping pills when I was younger, so it wasn't a stretch for me to imagine this scenario. I don't know if Mike knew this about me. Later, after Mike died from an overdose of pentobarbital, I wondered if he was baiting me with this question. Maybe Mike was just being cruel to me, knowing that August after Rob's wedding—just two months before Mike died—he was going to kill himself. Maybe he meant to leave me with a tinge of guilt.

At his funeral, one of Mike's friends told me that after Mike visited Indiana that weekend in August, he'd gotten on a plane and flown to Hong Kong. There, Mike bought a vial of liquid pentobarbital. He'd planned to do this long before he arrived at Rob's wedding, I tell myself now, long before we sat on that dock that hot August, long before we played that game. My answer to Mike's what-if question had nothing to do with his method of dying. But still, that what-if game haunts me.

Lily Bart's marriage prospects dry up. She gambles away what money she had at a party one weekend. Unmarried and penniless, Lily's prospects are dire. Her friends eventually spurn her—even Lawrence Selden—and she loses her place in Manhattan society. Eventually, she is reduced to working in a milliner's shop and living in a boardinghouse.

Her health fails her, too. Anxiety prevents her from sleeping. She looks to the future and she sees only gloom.

To seek relief, Lily visits a chemist, who gives her a bottle of chloral. The chemist, however, warns Lily that, "it's a queer-acting drug. A drop or two more, and off you go." Lily doesn't want to kill herself; she wants respite from thinking about the life she sees before her:

She had a sense of deeper empoverishment—of an inner destitution compared to which outward conditions dwindled into insignificance. It was indeed miserable to be poor—to look forward to a shabby, anxious middle-age, leading by dreary degrees of economy and self-denial to gradual absorption in the dingy communal existence of the boarding-house.

Lily wants to stop thinking about her past, and her present situation, and the dark future that she is presented with. She wants to sleep, to take that "brief bath of oblivion."

In his suicide note, Mike writes, "I fought so hard all my life to give myself the self-esteem I needed to survive emotionally as a gay man in this society, then to have a devastating disease come along & rob me of all my self worth is just too much." Mike looked to the future and he knew what was ahead of him. He'd witnessed scores of friends die of AIDS and knew what the virus did to a person's body: the way the muscles atrophy, the opportunistic diseases that the body's defenses cannot fight off, the weight loss, the dementia, the final months lying in bed unable to control one's bladder and bowels. The messiness of death. He saw his future and rather than face it, he took his own life, even if that horrible future was many, many years away.

In her boardinghouse room, Lily tries to forget her bleak situation. She sees before her the next day and the day after that and each one "swarmed about her like a shrieking mob." She wants one anxiety-free night. She wants to forget about her life.

As she did every night, she puts a few drops of the chloral in a glass of water. She knows the number of drops she can use safely, but that night she puts in a few more than were prescribed. She doesn't care. She wants to sleep and to forget. She drinks the concoction and turns out the light in her bedroom. The drug begins to take its affect:

The very slowness and hesitancy of the effect increased its fascination: it was delicious to lean over and look down into the dim abysses of unconsciousness. Tonight the drug seemed to work more slowly than usual: each passionate pulse had to be stilled in turn, and it was long before she felt them dropping into abeyance, like sentinels falling asleep at their posts.

Then, the drug takes over and "warmth flowed through her once more, she yielded to it, sank into it, and slept."

At the end of Mike's suicide note, his neat penmanship gave way to unintelligible scrawls. The pentobarbital was bubbling up in his stomach and slowing his heartbeat. He could not see the notepad clearly. He could not keep the pen steady. He lost the train of his thoughts and repeated himself: "You may not understand but I can't but so my heart's desire is to live in Indy & be married." Just before he fell to the floor unconscious, he lost the motor skills in his hand. The note ends with broken letters and confused syntax: "ou are very spal people th his &."

This is all I have left of Mike. All that I know of what happened in that hotel room in the Holiday Inn. This note that ends in gibberish. This note that barely makes sense to me when, even in the beginning, his handwriting is clear and precise. This note that fails to explain to me why he died, or how it felt to die. I have just his note, and it is not enough.

I wanted to have had the opportunity to save Mike. I wanted to know intuitively that he needed me, and I wanted to have run to him and helped him. I wanted our relationship to have been based on trust and honesty. I wanted him to have reached out to me and to have told me that he needed my help. I loved him, and I wanted love to have been enough to keep him alive.

In the last chapter of *The House of Mirth*, Lawrence Selden wakes up in the morning and realizes that he loves Lily, and no matter what reputation she has earned, and no matter what Manhattan society believed of her, Selden still loves her. Selden is beside himself with happiness; he feels "a youthful sense of adventure. He has cut loose from the familiar shores of habit, and launched himself on uncharted seas of emotion; all the old tests and measures were left behind, and his course was to be shaped by new stars."

Selden rushes to Lily's boardinghouse to tell her that he loves her, to plan out their futures together. When he gets there, however, he's surprised to see that his cousin is there. Selden realizes that something has happened to Lily.

Selden walks up the steps to Lily's room. He enters, and "though the blind was down, the irresistible sunlight poured a tempered golden flood into the room, and in its light Selden saw a narrow bed along the wall, and on the bed, with motionless hands and calm unrecognizing face, the semblance of Lily Bart." Selden goes and kneels by the bed, he bends over Lily's body, "draining their last moment to its lees; and in the silence there passed between them the word which made all clear."

Having reread *The House of Mirth*, my frame of reference has changed. I no longer see myself as Lily Bart. Instead, I see myself as Lawrence Selden. The one who finds it's too late to save the one he loves. The one who realizes he could've made all the difference if given the chance. The only one left to mourn the one he loves.

And in Lily, I see what Mike might have seen before he died. That need to get away from his present anxiety and the unbearable future. The one who looked into the abyss and found solace. The one who only needed rest but went too far and fell into that irretrievable bliss. The one I loved but who is no longer here.

Morta Sicura

David and I sat up in bed in the Pensione Mimosa, which was just down the street from the Pantheon in Rome. It was after dark in early February of 1993, and we were reading a paperback version of Hemingway's *The Sun Also Rises*. I'd read a page, tear it out of the book, and hand it to David. He'd read it and then place the page on his bedside table. I wasn't really reading the Hemingway—just scanning the pages—but it was a good distraction.

It was my idea to move to Rome, but it was David's dream. He'd taught architecture in Rome four years earlier and had been trying to get back. I'd met David five months earlier, and I liked the idea of being an expat, even though I wasn't an adventurous person.

Before we left the States, David had made plans for us to stay with his friend Mark until we found a job and settled in. David knew that Mark was ill—he'd been diagnosed with brain cancer—but Mark assured us that everything was fine with his health. The day before we flew to Rome, however, Mark's girlfriend Monica, who was a doctor, called to say that he'd taken a turn for the worse, and that it would be impossible for us to stay with him.

Mark died our first week in Rome. We stood in All-Saints Church—an Anglican church just down from Piazza del Popolo—to mourn him. Nine months later, David and I would stand in another church back in Indianapolis to mourn Mike.

Marcella, a woman we knew from a local *alimentari*, had made arrangements for us to stay at the pensione on credit. Marcella was a small woman with dark hair that she held back with barrettes.

I liked her because she spoke English—I didn't speak Italian. She assured the landlady at the pensione that David and I would pay our bill in full when we left.

The room at the Pensione Mimosa was large with two double beds that David and I pushed together in the evening, and then pulled apart in the morning so that the cleaning woman wouldn't see that we were sleeping together. To the left of the bed was a large porcelain sink with a brown water stain running from the cold-water tap down to the drain.

On the bed between us were a half-eaten loaf of bread, orange peels, and a bottle of water that we shared. This was all we could afford for dinner, but I hadn't eaten much. My stomach was tight and heavy as if it were filled with rocks.

We were smokers then. When we lived in the States, we smoked Marlboro Reds. In Rome, however, we couldn't afford American cigarettes and had to settle for the Italian brand MS, which was cheap and awful tasting. Officially, MS stood for *Monopolio Statale* (state monopoly)—the historical name came from the Latin, *Messis Summa* (best crop)—although this was a dramatic overstatement. Most Italians called MS *Merda Secca* (dried shit, which more accurately described the taste), or *Morta Sicura* (sure death, which was also an apt nickname).

The ashtrays on both of our nightstands were overfilled, which reminded me of the ashtray that sat on the side table of my father's La-Z-Boy. He too was a heavy smoker, and I remember my childhood home filled with smoke and used butts and the smell of nicotine.

We'd been in Rome for three weeks, and each day our situation grew worse. We knew that we couldn't pay the bill at the pensione, or, for that matter, afford another pack of cigarettes.

Earlier that day, while we sat on the steps of the fountain in front of the Pantheon scanning the want ads in the English newspaper, David suggested that I call Mike for help because Mike was in the best financial position to lend us money. It took me a long time to agree to David's suggestion. I'd spent my life trying to impress Mike, to make him proud of me. I hated the idea of having to admit that I'd failed.

David and I hadn't been together long enough for me to feel secure in our relationship. I didn't want to disagree with him about calling Mike because I was afraid David would leave me.

I wasn't the adventurous guy David assumed I was when we met. On our first date, I'd gone on about living a life of purpose and wonder: a romantic life I imagined living without ever having lived it. When we walked around Rome, David became frustrated with my lack of intellectual curiosity as we visited churches and he'd point out the Cimabue crucifixes and the Bernini statues and the Giotto frescos while I fidgeted next to him, wondering what time we were going to eat lunch.

I left the bread and the orange peels and the bottle of water on the bed, put my half of the Hemingway down, stubbed out my last cigarette of the night, and turned my back to David when I lay down to sleep. I couldn't sleep, though. My mind was too busy mulling over the phone conversation I'd have to have with Mike in the morning.

Mike and I were raised in a family of business people who knew the risk of lending money. Once, when I was between jobs and couldn't pay the rent, I'd asked Mike for help. He refused, echoing the lesson of our father that money lending promoted laziness and immorality.

I lay awake all night, knowing for certain that Mike wouldn't help us.

In the morning, David and I walked out of the pensione. David knew the way to the SIP office (the Italian phone company) in Piazza di San Silvestro. I was tired and irritable, though, and rather than follow David, I set off on my own. I turned left on Via Santa Chiara—the street where the pensione was located.

"It's this way," David said, standing in front of the pensione.

"No, it's not," I said over my shoulder without breaking stride.

I'm stubborn like my father. As soon as David said that I was going in the wrong direction, I knew that he was right. I kept walking in the wrong direction, however. When I came to the corner, I didn't have a clue which way to turn. Finally, I turned around and marched back to where David was standing.

"Let's go then," I said, extending my left arm as if I were being generous and allowing him to lead the way.

As we turned right on Via Santa Chiara and passed in front of the Pantheon, I stayed a few paces behind David. He led me through the Piazza di Monte Citorio where the Camera dei Deputati was located with its handsome *carabinieri* standing guard, and passed the heavily ornate column of Marcus Aurelius, and across the Via del Corso. On the other side of the Corso was the Rinascente department store where, when we first arrived and thought that money wouldn't be a problem, I bought my first article of Italian clothing—a blue dress shirt. Around the corner from the department store was Piazza di San Silvestro where buses idled between runs and taxis lined up waiting for fares.

The SIP office was on the far side of the piazza in a fortress–like building that had heavily rusticated walls and tall windows that were shielded with thick iron gates and large wooden entry doors filled with brass studs. I stood in the piazza for a little while, finishing my cigarette and getting up the courage to call Mike.

I didn't ask David to go inside the SIP office with me. I had to make the call by myself, I said, as if I were slipping into a confessional where the acts of contrition I'd be asked to make for my failures were mine alone.

Once inside the front doors of the SIP office, I walked along a corridor until I came to a bank of tellers behind a glass partition.

I was nervous and sweating when I approached the teller—a man not much older than me with thick black hair that was slicked back, and a couple of days' worth of stubble on his face. I said, "*Chiamo casa*," to him, which made me sound like a frightened first grader asking to call home. The teller dismissed my lame attempt to speak Italian with a swipe of his hand. In English, he asked for the number I wanted to call, and then calculated the cost for a five-minute conversation. I paid, and the teller pointed to a booth where he'd place the call.

Inside the booth, there was a small box that kept track of the time of the phone call. I waited until the phone rang and picked up the receiver. When I heard Mike's voice, I started crying uncontrollably while Mike asked several times who was calling. Fifteen seconds had ticked away on the timer before I could say a word.

When Mike and I were growing up, I was a sensitive boy who made our mother birthday cards with dried flowers and craft-paper butterflies glued to the front. I was always picked on by other boys—including my brothers—who called me a fag. I wanted Mike to have protected me, not because he was strong or knew how to fight, but because, I thought, he was empathetic. He wasn't, particularly.

Once, though, on my sixteenth birthday, Mike sent me a card with a picture of Van Gogh's *Irises* on the front. Inside the card, Mike had handwritten the lyrics to "Somewhere over the Rainbow," *the* anthem of the gay community. I hadn't picked up on this clue, however.

I kept that card for years as proof that Mike loved me.

As the first minute rolled off the clock in the phone booth, I told Mike that David and I were in Rome. I told him that we'd seen the Vatican and the Coliseum and more churches than I cared to remember.

Finally, I asked for the money—I only needed a couple of hundred dollars. Before Mike could say a word, I spent too much of my allotted time trying to convince him that I was good for the money, as if I were talking to a loan officer questioning my credit worthiness.

Mike sounded nonchalant. He said that he didn't have a problem giving me money. He even offered to wire me a thousand dollars.

"No need to pay me back," he said.

I was ecstatic. I spent the remaining balance of my time talking to him about being in Rome as if we were used to having casual conversations. Mike said that he had been to Rome many times. He spent a good part of our phone conversation giving me a list of restaurants that David and I could never afford to eat in.

Later, after Mike died, I understood that his generosity was less an empathetic act and more a divestiture of assets that people who are planning to kill themselves engage in.

By that winter—when David and I were in Rome—Mike knew that he was HIV positive. He'd found out six months earlier.

Because of Mike's money, we were able to stay in Rome a little while longer, enough time for me to find a job teaching in an American high school in Arezzo, a small Tuscan town two and a half hours north of Rome. We had to return to the States, however, while the school processed my visa.

My Italian work visa took much longer than the school had assured me it would. We returned to the States in early March of 1993. We assumed that we'd be back in Italy by early that summer, but we hadn't yet appreciated the slow pace at which the Italian government moves.

While we were back in the States, David and I were invited to a memorial service for a man we barely knew who'd died from AIDS. We felt like interlopers at the service and spent most of our time walking around with a drink in our hand and making small talk.

As we were about to leave the memorial service, a woman came up to us. She was thin with wild grey hair. She was enthusiastic to see us, as if we'd been long-lost friends who'd met up again by chance.

"You're angels," she said to us, grabbing our forearms.

We hadn't done anything angelic except show up and give our respects. We thanked her and tried to get loose from her grasp.

"No, really," she said. "I can see angels, and you two are radiant angels."

We thought that she'd had too much to drink. We laughed. She frowned.

"I'm dead serious," she said. "You don't have to believe me, but you're angels. Real angels."

We stopped laughing, nodded our heads dutifully, and removed her hand from our forearms before making an exit.

A few months later—at the end of October—Mike died.

Then my work visa came through, and David and I returned to Italy.

Of all the documents concerning Mike's death that I've looked at in order to come to terms with my grief, his death certificate is the most benign and the saddest. The certificate was filed on October 29, 1993, but not released until February 4, 1994, after the autopsy had been done and the toxicology report had been issued.

The certificate is an 8½ × 11 sheet of embossed stationery with a royal blue border etched with oak leaves. In the bottom left corner is the seal of the City of New York and in the bottom right corner is the seal of the Department of Health and Mental Hygiene.

The header reads "Death Transcript" as if this were a record of some accomplishment Mike received in school, a commendation for having completed a life that he found so difficult.

His death has a number: 156-93-060219.

His name is squarely typed out: Michael   J.   Barnes.

It's one of the last times, I imagine, his name will appear on a document that attests to his having lived. It will no longer be written out on invitations to weddings or anniversaries or dinner parties. It will no longer be printed on the envelopes of utility bills or bank statements or pieces of junk mail. It will no longer be recorded on census rolls or voting records or apartment leases. It will barely be inscribed in letters between friends or family. His name will disappear, I fear, as if he never existed.

Below his name, the certificate records the place of his death—Manhattan, 1605 Broadway—and the date and time—October 28, 1993, at 3:12 P.M.. It gives his sex and his age: Male, 34 years.

In the section that records the cause of his death, it states: "Acute intoxication by the combined effects of pentobarbital, ethanol, quinine, sertraline, nortriptyline and diphenhydramine." A cocktail of poison that he'd read about, I'd learned later, in a book published by the Hemlock Society.

The certificate gives the manner of death as suicide, and the medical examiner firmly affixes his signature, vowing that, "on the basis of examination and/or investigation, in my opinion, death occurred due to the cause and manner stated."

At the bottom of the certificate, under the heading Personal Particulars, the certificate lists Mike's address in Manhattan on E. Eleventh Street, his birthdate, social security number, and his occupation. It also lists my parents' names, and the address where they live in Indianapolis—the same house in which we grew up.

Finally, the certificate gives the location where my brother is buried: Oaklawn Memorial Gardens, which sounds peaceful and contemplative, like a place where the worries of everyday life can be forgotten.

By the time the death certificate was issued, David and I had moved into our apartment in Arezzo. I taught in the American high school just up the road, and David worked at an Italian architecture firm.

While we lived in Italy, I talked about Mike constantly. I spoke his name every chance I could until his story became one of the many stories I told about my past. But I hadn't really grieved for Mike. The stories I told were anecdotes that prevented me from sitting quietly and allowing sorrow to run its course.

Before he died, Mike had introduced us to an Italian friend, whom he'd met while studying abroad in Angers, France, during his junior year in college. Nicoletta (or Nikki) was from a wealthy family that had ancestral ties to the old Italian monarchy. Her family's home was in Milan but they had a villa just outside of Genoa and an impressive palazzo in the town of Sarteano, seventy kilometers south of Arezzo.

Within our first two months in Arezzo, Nikki came to visit.

David and I lived outside the city walls of Arezzo in the *periferia*, out past the hospital in a neighborhood dubbed *zona Americana* where other faculty and administrators from the school lived. Our apartment was in a nondescript modern building on

Via Poggio Bracciolini. We lived on the first floor. Above us were two other apartments that were occupied by young Italian couples: Gianni and Silvia, who both had black hair and wore glasses, and who were as sharp to each other as were their facial features; and Mauro, who was tall and handsome and sweet, and his wife Elena, who was petite and quiet.

Nikki arrived on a Friday. When she pulled up in front of the apartment in her blue Peugeot, she bounded out of the car to greet us. She was a big woman, and wore an overstuffed North Face jacket, thick wool herringbone pants, and a knit cap. She had on gaudy makeup: sparkling green eye shadow, heavy rouge, and bright red lipstick. She wasn't much older than David and me, but she looked like my great aunt Nell whose heavily perfumed house I visited as a kid at Easter.

I chuckled when I saw Nikki, not because she looked clownish, but because she looked exactly like someone Mike would befriend. When he lived in New York, Mike had an eccentric group of friends, who were completely opposite of the boring and predictable people we knew growing up in our middle-class, Midwestern neighborhood. Nikki embodied Mike's fantasy of growing up in a privileged household that could trace its lineage back to kings and emperors and popes, when our ancestors where laborers and boilermakers and railroad men.

Nikki stopped short when she first saw me. I knew that I looked like Mike—people had been telling me this my entire life. At Mike's funeral, his friends, who'd never met me, had the same shocked reaction as Nikki had.

David pushed forward and greeted Nikki with a handshake and a friendly smile. She hugged him, while continuing to stare at me over his shoulder, trying to determine if I was real or not.

When she decided that I wasn't a figment of her imagination, she came over and hugged me tightly. "*Caro,*" she cried into my ear. "*Caro, caro, caro!*"

David unloaded her car, remarking on the amount of food she'd brought: an enormous *coppa*, dried sausages, wheels of cheese, loaves of bread, freshly pressed olive oil from her family's orchards, and bottles of wine from their vineyard.

She'd also brought a small TV, which we hadn't asked for. (Later, in the afternoons when I'd come home from school, I'd watch the game show *Il Grande Gioco dell'Oca* on Nikki's TV in a feeble attempt to learn Italian.)

David struggled to carry the load into the apartment, while Nikki grabbed my arm and leaned heavily against me as I escorted her inside. In the apartment, she threw off her coat and her hat and took a quick look around. I lit a cigarette and took a long drag on it.

Compared to the places Nikki was used to staying, the apartment in Arezzo was small. We had an entryway with a credenza on which sat a lamp and a telephone. In the front room there was a couch, dining table, chairs, and a breakfront. We had one bathroom with a washing machine in it. There were two bedrooms, one that we used for guests—although except for Nikki, we had no guests. Our bedroom had two double beds that we pushed together—not having to worry about pulling them apart in the morning—a wardrobe, chest of drawers and two nightstands. We had a small kitchen with a green Formica table where we ate all of our meals. Off the kitchen was a terrace where a washing sink was located and a clothesline that stretched from one side of the terrace to the other. The floors of the apartment were a terrazzo marble, as were the floors of the apartments above us, across which Silvia and Elena shuffled in their house slippers in order to keep the marble polished, as all Italian housewives did.

After giving an obligatory compliment on the apartment, Nikki decamped into the kitchen to prepare food for a party that I knew wasn't going to take place.

She put a large pot of water on the stove to make polenta and asked me to slice the *coppa*, which smelled raw and organic, like the inside of a good butcher shop. David was in the entryway phoning some of his colleagues to see if they'd drop by.

In the kitchen, Nikki launched into a series of lessons on how to survive in Italy. She explained that the old women in the neighborhood knew everything that went on, and that I wouldn't be able to get away with anything. David and I already knew this. We were two men living together, and our Italian neighbors took a special interest in us. I didn't understand what trouble Nikki thought I'd get into, however. Perhaps, she thought I was prone to throwing loud parties or likely to invite strange men over to the apartment or make a fool of myself stumbling home drunk in the early hours of the morning. Perhaps, she had an idea that I was like Mike in these ways.

In reality, though, the only curiosity I aroused in the neighborhood was when I hung laundry out on the line or stood in the kitchen cooking. Then, the women in our neighborhood—especially Silvia and Elena—pointed at their husbands and said that it *was* possible for a man to do household chores.

Being Milanese, Nikki explained the difference between northern and southern Italians, drawing her finger across the kitchen table to demarcate the dairy line on an imaginary map where her countrymen north of Rome cooked with butter while her cousins in the south cooked with oil. This difference, she said, was not just about food, but rather about temperament and tolerance: the more sophisticated (and wealthier) northerners and the cruder (and poorer) southerners. I'd be safe up north, she said, but less so in the south.

She told me to be distrustful of Italian men because they had their reputations to consider, and to be wary of German tourists because . . . well . . . she said, they were German.

The olive oil that Nikki had brought us was cloudy, unlike the clear oil we bought at the store. Nikki explained that this was the sign of good olive oil, a true Italian olive oil that still contained its sediment. Let it stand for a couple of months, Nikki said, and the oil would settle. Unlike her advice about being well behaved, and her theory of northern and southern Italians, and her prejudice against German tourists, Nikki's lesson on olive oil was accurate.

As Nikki waited for the water to boil, and I sliced the *coppa*, she told me all of this in one long string of sentences that never seemed to end. At first I thought her chatter was a sign of her being nervous to meet us for the first time, but David and I came to understand that it was a particularly annoying trait of Nikki's.

Nikki never stopped talking—not that entire weekend, or on a trip we took with her to Lago Trasimeno a few weeks later, or when we met her for dinner, or when we visited her in Sarteano toward the end of that spring. Her constant talking filled the space around her as if she were trying to protect herself in a cocoon of words.

David came into the kitchen shaking his head to tell me that he couldn't convince anyone from his office to drop by for dinner. The invitation was simply too late.

Nikki stood over the pot of boiling water and very slowly poured in the grains of polenta. She wore a fuzzy green sweater. As she stood in front of the stove and stirred the pot, I noticed a thread hanging down from her sleeve, swaying in the air as if the thread was trying to detach itself from Nikki and float down onto the kitchen floor.

David pulled out a pack of MS and offered Nikki one. She chided him, pointing instead to her pack of Gitanes. She said they were the only brand we should smoke. We could never afford them on our salaries. They were better cigarettes, of course. They were French after all, and Nikki—as with all Milanesi—associated herself with the French more than with Italians.

While David and Nikki smoked their Gitanes, I slipped into the entryway and made a few phone calls to my coworkers in the neighborhood. I convinced them to stop over for a drink if they couldn't also have dinner with us. A few of them reluctantly agreed.

When my coworkers arrived, Nikki greeted them as she might greet a dignitary visiting one of her villas. My coworkers were nonplussed by her appearance and her behavior. They stayed for no more than fifteen minutes—enough time to have a glass of wine, a slice of coppa, and some cheese. When they made their excuses to leave, Nikki was beside herself. She complained that it was a great insult to come and go so quickly. They hurried away.

In the end, it was only the three of us for dinner. Nikki cried. She imagined the party as a kind of gala where we'd introduce her to our friends, and they, of course, would be impressed by her obvious pedigree.

In the morning, Nikki packed up her things in order to head down to Sarteano where, she told us, she was having dinner with a few of her cousins.

When I escorted Nikki to her car, I hugged her goodbye and said that I looked forward to her next visit. She held on to me tightly and whispered into my ear, "You know the Indians killed him, don't you?"

These words didn't register with me. They were just a string of words in a never-ending string of words that she'd brought with her that weekend. I was tired of hearing her voice, which was pitched an octave above annoying, and let these words slip away as easily as I wanted her to slip away.

I nodded as if I agreed with Nikki. She kissed David on the cheeks, said, "*Ciao*," and zipped away.

A month later, David and I took the train down to Nikki's palazzo in Sarteano. Like Arezzo, Sarteano is a walled town in the Tuscan hills. Nikki's palazzo was on the main square. It was an impressive house with views of the Val d'Orcia. She took us to an expensive restaurant for lunch, and as with her initial visit in Arezzo, she spent all of our time together talking, giving us lessons and warnings about living in Italy: the outrageous price of utilities, the dangers of driving on the autostrada, the way some local merchants cheated tourists and expats.

When Nikki dropped us off at the train station after lunch, she once again hugged me and whispered into my ear, "The Indians killed him."

This time, I caught what she'd said. I was so taken aback by the absurdity of the idea that I stepped away from her. I couldn't figure out what she meant. Indians? What?

I thought for a moment that Nikki knew something about Mike's death that I didn't. While I hadn't yet seen Mike's death certificate, I had been to the morgue in New York to identify his body and knew that he'd committed suicide because the police and medical examiner had told me he had. I knew that Mike was HIV positive and that in his suicide note he blamed his diagnosis for robbing him of his life. I knew from his friends that he was an addict of either drugs or alcohol, or both. I knew that he hated being gay. I knew that his death had devastated me, even if while we lived in Italy I tried as hard as I could to keep that devastation at bay.

"Mike died of an overdose," I said to Nikki, still perplexed by why she'd say such a thing.

"No, no, Caro," she said, shaking her head. "He was killed by Indians."

I didn't know how to counter what she'd said. None of it made sense to me. Perhaps, I wanted to believe her, as if it would be easier to accept Mike's death if he'd been killed by Indians rather than having killed himself.

We said goodbye to Nikki, walked into the station, and boarded the train back to Arezzo.

I didn't know what to make of Nikki. She was strange and she talked too much, that was obvious. But I hadn't yet realized that she was also crazy.

A few weeks later, Nikki called to say that she'd made dinner reservations. She wanted to introduce us to family friends who lived in Arezzo.

We met Nikki at Pizzeria Al Parco, which was just down the street from the train station in Arezzo. David and I had been there a number of times. The food was good, and we liked the hostess, who was tall and had bleached-blonde hair that she kept cropped close to her scalp.

Nikki introduced David and me to her friends: Alberto and Carla, a glamorous couple—he with his dark hair and Van Dyke beard and she with her *bella figura*—and Guigliermo and Barbara, who were warm and familiar in the way good people are. Carla and Guigliermo had grown up with Nikki.

Nikki began speaking the minute we met her at the restaurant. Her talking, however, didn't seem to bother her friends. They simply talked over her so that while David and I talked to Nikki's friends—who turned out to be very nice people—Nikki maintained a steady monologue as if she were talking to someone else completely: an invisible friend, I thought.

A month later, Alberto and Carla invited us to their apartment for dinner. They lived in a modern apartment building near the Stadio Comunale. Their apartment overlooked the soccer fields.

During this subsequent dinner, Carla gave us a little of Nikki's history.

Nikki was an only child whose mother died when Nikki was young. Her father was still alive but he was frail. He worried that when he died there'd be no one to look after Nikki, who needed looking after. She wasn't well, as we'd come to realize, and had suffered a number of mental breakdowns. She'd been in and out of hospitals. Family and friends were concerned that she belonged in a long-term care facility, but that her father would never commit her. They also knew that the chances of Nikki taking her own life were great, but no one seemed to be able to do anything about it.

It was a difficult story to hear.

After Mike's suicide, I regretted that I never had the chance to save him. I don't know what I could have done, but I wanted to have had the possibility of doing something.

It was so difficult to be around Nikki that when we were with her, we couldn't wait until she was gone. Contrary to the woman who believed David and I were angels, I didn't feel any empathy for Nikki. Rather, I was annoyed that Mike had left her with us. She wasn't my problem, I told myself, especially since her family and friends were well aware of her mental state.

In late April of 1994, the cold dampness of winter evaporated and a field of red poppies bloomed in an empty lot at the end of our street. The neighborhood smelled of fennel and figs. In a few weeks, school would be out for the summer, and David and I could begin taking side trips to Venice and Milan, and back to Rome.

One afternoon, after I'd returned from teaching and while David was still at work, I got a call from Nikki. She couldn't stop crying. In between sobs she said, "The Indians tried to kill me." When she calmed down a little, she told me that she'd been driving in Milan and the Indians had tried to run her off the road. They'd been following her for months, she said, and they were intent on killing her the way they'd killed Mike.

I wanted to be kind to Nikki, thinking that if I could do nothing else for her, I could at least be kind. I tried to be compassionate and reassuring. I tried to think of something practical to do like call Carla or Guigliermo and let them know what had happened. But I wasn't kind or compassionate or reassuring. I did nothing to help her.

I'd grown tired of Nikki. Her incessant talking drove me nuts. While at first I thought that her insane theory that Mike had been killed by Indians might lessen my grief, it now felt as if she were making fun of Mike's death.

"Mike poisoned himself," I hissed at Nikki over the phone. "He fucking killed himself. Can't you get that through your crazy head?"

She whimpered as if she suddenly felt a sharp pain in her gut.

"It was the Indians," she repeated. She'd stopped crying and her voice become soft, as if she'd resigned herself to not being understood. "The Indians killed him," she whispered. Then, she hung up the phone.

When I put down the receiver, I was trembling. Nikki's call had made me angry. I wasn't an angry person. My father was an angry man whose anger flowed just below the surface and boiled over at unexpected moments: when dinner was late, when someone (me) had used his best pen, when he found out that two of his sons were gay, and when one of them had killed himself. But I wasn't my father. I didn't inherit his temperament, I told myself—and continue to tell myself.

After hanging up with Nikki, I went into the front room of the apartment, sat down on the couch, and lit a cigarette. It took chain-smoking three MS's before I could calm down.

Over the coming months and years, Nikki would call or drop a letter in the mail, but I never returned her calls or answered her letters. Instead, I let her slip away until all communication between us stopped.

In the end, I don't know what happened to Nikki. Perhaps she'd finally been institutionalized. It was more likely that she died. Perhaps, she'd taken her own life, thinking it was better to die than be constantly chased by her phantom Indians.

Nine months after we moved to Arezzo, the school at which I worked became insolvent and closed its doors. I didn't have the fortitude or the wherewithal to find another job. Instead, I gave up and returned to the States—David stayed behind in Italy for a couple of months before joining me in New York.

In giving up on living an expat's life, I felt as if I'd disappointed Mike, who'd saved me when I called him from Rome looking for money. In giving up on Nikki, I felt as if I'd similarly failed him. But what did it matter, I told myself. Mike was dead, and regardless of why or how he died, the transcript of his death had foreclosed all other possibilities.

Almost every year, David and I return to Rome. We've established ourselves in New York now, and the time we spend in Rome is far less hectic and desperate than that first time. We have the luxury to stay in nice hotels and eat out at good restaurants. We have the time to stroll casually through the cobbled streets and marvel at a city that we've come to see as our second home.

Living in New York, I feel Mike everywhere, as if he isn't dead but simply away. In Rome, I feel the loss of him less sharply. My grief, however, is still with me. It's become part of me like a vital organ that I can't live without.

When we are in Rome, we drop by the *alimentari* to visit Marcella. We walk past the Pantheon and All-Saints Church and over to the Pensione Mimosa. We remember those horrible cigarettes we once smoked. We think of Nikki and Mike and the phantom creatures that haunted them. And I tell myself, "It's good to be alive."

Acknowledgments

Writing this book, I have depended upon a few key theorists and historians to understand suicide and its lasting ramifications on those of us who survive. In particular, Simon Critchley's aptly titled book *Suicide* allowed me to read Mike's suicide note as a last-ditch effort to find a viable identity. Similarly, Adam Phillips's work in *Unforbidden Pleasures* (and especially the chapter "Against Self-Criticism") helped me to see the destructive nature of my own self-criticism that, at times, has left me as vulnerable to suicide as Mike was.

Both Critchley and Phillips—as with most suicidologists—depend upon Freud's famous essay, "Mourning and Melancholia," which in turn studies Hamlet's famous "To be or not to be" soliloquy in Shakespeare's *Hamlet*. Both Freud's and Shakespeare's texts focus on the self-protecting ego that should give us pause when we are faced with the "slings and arrows of outrageous fortune," but which for some collapses under the weight of simply living.

A. Alvarez's important and well-known book *The Savage God: A Study of Suicide* was also important in writing this book. Along with Georges Minois's *History of Suicide: Voluntary Death in Western Culture* (trans. Lydia G. Cochrane), Alvarez provides a historical context for suicide from Dante to Dada.

I want to acknowledge the mentors who made this book possible. *The Dark Eclipse* was my thesis project for my Masters of Fine Arts in Creative Writing at Bennington College. First and foremost, I am indebted and forever grateful to Susan Cheever, who inspired the writing of this book, and especially its use of source documents to get at Mike's death. In addition, Benjamin Anastas, Sven Birkerts, and Peter Trachtenberg contributed greatly in shaping these essays.

I would like to thank the class of January 2017 from the MFA program at Bennington College, and those workshop peers who read many of these essays and gave valuable feedback. I am grateful to the Pratt Institute for accommodating my needs to pursue my MFA and write this book.

I also would like to thank Ken Corbett, for giving me the space and the time to mark where the dark eclipses be, and to explore that strange combination of love and absence and despair.

I have been fortunate to have worked with and been supported by amazing writers, intellectuals, and all-around good people, including Alice Friman, Ira Livingston, Ellery Washington, James Hannaham, Samantha Hunt, Mendi Obadike, Jennifer Miller, Macarena Gómez-Barris, Jack Halberstam, Gregg Horowitz, Brad Gooch, Edward Burns, Marina Budhos, L. H. McMillin, and Susann Cokal. To Greg Clingham and the staff at Bucknell University Press, thank you for seeing the value in publishing this book. And to the staff at Rutgers University Press, thank you for seeing this book through to its publication.

I owe a tremendous amount of thanks to Therese Eiben, who has read more of my work than almost anyone else. And to her husband George Milling-Stanley, a reader of such breadth and variety that only his knowledge of music outshines it.

To Nancy Foley, who, when Mike died, stepped in to fill a void that I thought would never heal. And to Diane Schneider for liking roller-coasters as much as I do. To K. C. and Barbara and John. (To Jack and MaryLou.)

To my mother, who suffered a far greater loss than I did.

Even to those places and those people and those circumstances that were difficult to endure, but which have made me the person— and the writer —that I have become.

Finally, I don't know how to thank my husband, David Foley. The man I dared to love, and the man who dared to love me back.

About the Author

A. W. BARNES has a PhD in English literature and an MFA in creative writing. His nonfiction has appeared in *Broad Street*, *Away Journal*, *Gertrude Press*, and *Sheepshead Review*. His academic book *Post-Closet Masculinities in Early Modern England* was published by Bucknell University Press in 2009.